HEALING THE WOUNDS OF DIVORCE

reader to understand the devastation and pain that a divorce can bring. This book is a great resource for those that are hurting and traumatized and has several important steps to help the reader regain their self-confidence and happiness. She expertly explains the benefits of self-care and having the support of friends. There is information of recovering from the grief stages of divorce and the impact of divorce on your children. The best part of this book is that shows how to get back to YOU! I recommend this book for anyone going through a divorce as a resource for self-help."

—**Dr. S. Craig DPT**, Author of *To Pee or Not to Pee? The Guide for Reducing and Eliminating Urinary Incontinence*

"Freda Wilson's book, *Healing the Wounds of Divorce* gives readers a compassionate and thorough road map for how to remedy the pain and alienation that so often accompanies divorce. Reverend Wilson shares her own story with bold honesty and offers readers a way to reconnect with themselves and God. The book's healing framework is comprehensive and includes the need to grieve, to connect with children, to seek support and to stay true to oneself. Reverend Wilson leaves no stone unturned in offering those suffering from the wounds of divorce a way to find their best selves in the long run. As a psychotherapist, I recommend this book to anyone who needs a lifeline. In *Healing the Wounds of Divorce*, Freda Wilson gives you one!"

—**Amy R. Carpenter, LCSW, CYI**
Author of *Be Strong, Be Wise in the Age of #MeToo: The College Student's Guide to Sexual Safety*

HEALING
—— THE ——
WOUNDS
—— OF ——
DIVORCE

*How to Move on Healthier,
Happier, and More Fulfilled*

FREDA R. WILSON

NEW YORK

LONDON • NASHVILLE • MELBOURNE • VANCOUVER

HEALING THE WOUNDS OF DIVORCE
How to Move on Healthier, Happier, and More Fulfilled

© 2021 FREDA R. WILSON

Published in New York, New York, by Morgan James Publishing in partnership with Difference Press. Morgan James is a trademark of Morgan James, LLC.
www.MorganJamesPublishing.com

ISBN 978-1-63195-160-2 paperback
ISBN 978-1-63195-161-9 eBook
ISBN 978-1-63195-162-6 audio
Library of Congress Control Number: 2020907865

Cover Design Concept:
Jennifer Stimson

Cover Design:
Rachel Lopez, www.r2cdesign.com

Editor:
Cory Hott

Book Coaching:
The Author Incubator

Morgan James is a proud partner of Habitat for Humanity Peninsula and Greater Williamsburg. Partners in building since 2006.

Get involved today! Visit
www.MorganJamesBuilds.com

*This book is dedicated to all former pastors'
wives in the Christian church and all women
getting over a broken relationship or divorce.*

TABLE OF CONTENTS

FOREWORD

"I've known Freda for a number of years as a valuable member of our faith community, long-time ministry leader, and a personal friend. I know her story—one of deep pain and hurt. I also know that through it all, she has walked graciously with Jesus. In *Healing the Wounds of Divorce,* Freda writes from a place of deep love for God and God's people. Drawing from her own personal experience, she shares some valuable insights on, among many others, self-care, forgiveness, and building a community. *Healing* will give you hope that health and wholeness is God's desire for you."

—**James Grogan**, Lead Pastor, Eastlake Church
Catalyst Leader, San Diego Church Plant Movement

Chapter 1

INTRODUCTION

When you got married, I imagine you were in love and happy and looking forward to a life that would bring growth, maybe children, and the fulfillment of all the dreams and plans you both shared. But now that the marriage is over, you wonder what life will be like without him. Though you are in the throes of a painful and difficult season in your life, you can take this situation and turn it around so that it becomes your great opportunity to become creative and build a life that you will love and enjoy. You have numerous choices and the freedom to do, as you desire without opposition. You may be grieving the life you had with your ex, but as you grieve you can build an awesome new life. Novelist and poet Ben Okri says, "The most authentic thing about us is our capacity to create, to overcome, to endure, to transform, to love and to be greater than our suffering." You can be greater than the pain and challenges you are experiencing.

Meet Connie, a divorced mother with two minor children living at home. Connie was born in the Midwest and met her husband, Michael Pearson, as a young woman in her early twenties. Michael was soon to take over his father's church and decided he should get married before he took on his new position. He proposed to Connie and they married and moved to Dallas, Texas, to start their new lives as a pastor and first lady at the Kingdom Church. She and Michael became role models for their families, the church family, and the Christian community in Dallas. They were both dedicated to serving God's people at The Kingdom Church. Michael was a gifted, charismatic preacher and leader and the people loved him. Connie tried hard to fit into the new community and was learning the dos and don'ts of the pastor's wife. She was quite the fashionista and beautiful, and she enjoyed wearing her makeup, fashionable jewelry, and stylish clothing. She was surprised to learn that the older women in the church were not fond of her bold-colored lipstick, flashy jewelry, and modern clothing. She toned down the makeup and wore more conservative clothing to please the church mothers so that she could be liked and fit in.

As the first lady, Connie was expected to fulfill many roles. She was to volunteer wherever there was a need to support her husband. She was never a public speaker, but it soon became an expectation, so she learned to overcome her fear of speaking and singing in front of people and began working with the women of the church, preaching and teaching at various women's events and singing in the choir.

With all the growth and notoriety they experienced, Michael became more popular and busier in the church and the community, and that required extended hours at the church with his assistant, Sharon, and more time away from home. Since Connie also found herself just as busy volunteering in the church, and attending meetings she did not think too much about it at the time. She was, however, concerned that Michael was making decisions to exclude her from meetings with the female guest speakers they invited to speak at the church, an activity they normally shared. She was also excluded from some of the ministry and leadership activities.

Because of the distance that was growing between them, and Michael's changed behavior she began to question all the time he was spending away from home. One day at the office, she overheard inappropriate conversations between Michael and his assistant and her heart sank. She did not know what to say or do. She was so stunned, though in the back of her mind her intuition told her something was not right. She eventually asked Michael about what she heard and he denied it. "Connie, you are imagining things," he said, and acted as though he was upset that she would even approach him about something like that.

Knowing what she heard and the distance between them, Connie was worried, hurt, and sad. She had no one to speak with or vent to because everyone she associated with was in the church and her family was far away in the Midwest, and she did not want to get them involved. Because of their church background, secular counseling was frowned upon, so she had to struggle through her depression, hoping things would improve. She had no outlet, so all she could do was pray and cry in private. She was lonely, as is often the case for a pastor's wife.

Unwilling to let what she had heard between Michael and Sharon go, Connie looked through Michael's emails hoping to find something that would corroborate what she had heard and was thinking, and she did. She found sexually explicit emails between Michael and Sharon, and she was hurt and angry all at the same time. She confronted Michael again and well, as it turns out, Michael had been having an affair with his assistant Sharon for a few years. Michael apologized and begged for Connie's forgiveness, saying he would end the affair.

Connie forgave Michael, and told him Sharon had to leave the church and could no longer work for him if they were going to have a chance at mending the marriage. The following Sunday, while Michael and Connie were in one of the waiting areas in the back of the sanctuary, Connie saw Sharon come into the church and sit in the first row. She asked Michael, "Why is Sharon here?" He responded that she was a member and should not be prevented from attending church services. Connie became very angry and told Michael how disrespected she felt. Infuriated about Sharon being at church, Connie snapped and slapped Michael across his face and kept hitting him, leaving scratches on his face. She then walked into the sanctuary toward Sharon to confront her, but was stopped by a couple of deacons and was brought back into the room with Michael in the back of the church. They made it through the church service and a leadership meeting was scheduled the following week.

Connie told the church leaders and some of the members about the affair between Michael and Sharon. Michael apologized and asked for their forgiveness. He said he was truly sorry and regretted his behavior, and he assured them that the affair had ended. After the meeting Michael disappeared and was not in communication with Connie, the children, or the church for more than six months. Connie had no idea where Michael was or who he was with or what he was doing. She spoke with his parents and visited them over the Christmas holiday and was told to give him a little more time and he'd come around.

The members blamed Connie for the pastor leaving. They were upset about how she handled things and all the confusion that ensued. They were hurt and disappointed by everything that had happened. The membership declined while Michael was away, but Connie and the children continued to attend every week, thinking Michael would eventually return.

Since Michael was not at the church, the mortgage on their house was not paid. He did not send any money home for Connie and the children, and since Connie was not on the church's payroll, she could not pay the mortgage. She did ask the church leaders for financial support to pay the bills, but they said no since Michael was not there. She could not believe they would offer no financial assistance for her and the children.

Eventually, they lost the house and Connie was forced to move into an apartment. She was so distressed, as Michael was her first love, and she loved him and their life together. She ruminated over questions like how could he mess up their twenty-year fairy tale marriage and destroy their family? How could he be in love with someone else and think it was okay? She hoped Michael would return and work on the marriage.

Eventually, Connie and Michael talked. Michael returned and lived with Connie and the children in the apartment and he officially resigned from the church. They attended other churches about an hour's drive out of the city on Sunday mornings. They would talk about their life and ministry and tried to work through things, but it was difficult. Things were not the same between them. In an attempt to give an explanation for why he had the affair, he told Connie that he expected God to call her home because he believed he was going to marry Sharon. She wondered if he had planned to kill her or if he really believed she would die so he could be with Sharon. She could not believe what she heard.

Michael eventually said he did not want a wife who did ministry anymore. Connie couldn't believe it. After forcing her to do so many things over the years, he did not want it anymore. Is he loosing his mind she thought? With all the stress in their lives, intimacy became a problem for them because Connie was not enjoying sex with Michael. She was still battling thoughts about his affair and was turned off by the weight he had gained. Things never did get better. Connie felt that Michael did not want to be with her and was only there out of obligation.

Michael and Connie eventually divorced, and Connie tried to figure out what to do with her life. She was battling depression and so many different emotions. She found herself missing Michael and the things they shared. She missed the life they had and wondered if she would ever have the same fulfillment in ministry and if she would ever find love again.

She constantly worried about what choices to make for her future, and wondering how she would know if she was making the right decisions was a heavy burden. She didn't know how would she keep it all together and if God still had a great mission for her. What was God saying about all that had happened, she'd ask.

She tried hosting a few ministry events with some of the women she remained connected with after the divorce. She joined a local church and was licensed as a minister, but she still felt unsettled and had no clear understanding of what her purpose in life was without Michael, or what she should be doing with her life and in the church. She felt as though she was just chasing after the wind with no clear destination in view.

Connie was still grieving the loss of her marriage and the ministry she and Michael had at the Kingdom church. She never worked through all the hurt and anger she had when she found out about the affair and during Michael's extended months away from home. She had stuffed her feelings inside and did her best to ignore them, trying to remain strong for her and the children. She did not want to deal with the pain and crazy emotions.

If Connie is to be free of the hurt, anger, betrayal, and other emotions, she has to acknowledge how she is feeling, face the emotions and work through them. Otherwise she will take those bottled-up emotions that keep her connected to her past into other relationships making those relationships difficult and challenging. As she works through them, she can plan, set goals, focus on building positive self-esteem as a single woman, and build a renewed relationship with God that is centered on her and her future with Him. If she gets some emotional and spiritual support and guidance to help her face her emotions and work through how she is feeling, she can begin healing and letting go of her emotional bond to the past. In time, with the proper spiritual support she can find some spiritual clarity, develop some internal strength to make confident decisions about her life, and be empowered to move on healthier, happier, and more fulfilled.

Going through a divorce or a major breakup can be devastating and filled with excruciating pain. Overcoming this loss requires deliberate action, persistence and support. I've walked a similar walk as Connie when my marriage to a pastor ended painfully. After several years of grieving, working with support systems, and doing the inner work of facing the painful emotions that continued to cling to me, I was eventually able to move on and build a new life, a beautiful life that I enjoy immensely.

Chapter 2

MY JOURNEY THROUGH DIVORCE

I 've shared many details about my life in hopes of inspiring you to believe that you too can overcome difficult challenges and know joy and happiness. I am truly enjoying my life and all the many successes I've had. I am healthy, happy and strong. I have made it through some tough times and beaten many odds. It's been hard work, but the rewards are so worth it. I know that you can do the same.

I had no positive role models to teach me how to be wise and safe when dating when I was a young girl growing into a young woman. No one modeled how the dating life of a single female should look and there were no conversations where wisdom was shared about what to look for—good or bad—to aid me in making wise choices when dating. I did learn indirectly that having sex without being married was something that should not happen. I learned this in church as I was growing up and indirectly from my mom, who had traditional values from being raised in the South by my grandparents who were both devout Christians and leaders in the Christian church.

I observed my older sisters and their dating practices which mostly took place in secret, at least hidden from my mother, father, and stepmother, and they involved going places without permission, sometimes staying out all night, and running away or staying away for extended periods. My mother would be worried and furious, yelling and fussing, and sometimes whipping them and placing them on punishment. She called my dad in the middle of the night once because one of my sisters had not made it home. Dad came over and the police were called. She eventually came home—was dropped off by a guy at daybreak—and faced the wrath of my mom and dad.

One of my sisters would take me with her over her boyfriend's house and we'd hang out for hours. I also visited her in college while I was in high school and learned and observed many things. On one of my visits my boyfriend went, and of course my parents never knew he was with us. One sister would sneak to parties and dated some guys that

I did not like because of their questionable character and behavior in the neighborhood. We did not have the benefit of growing up with both of our biological parents in the home to secure us with unconditional love and shared, balanced discipline in our cultivation that was needed for teenage girls in Chicago's inner city. Having one biological parent at home or two parents, one being a stepparent, was a challenge for all of us in different ways, which I believe contributed to some of the rebellious behavior. At my mother's house, we behaved as we did because Dad was not there to enforce the correct behavior. One of my sisters perhaps acted out because she felt she was not being loved, and was being treated too strictly by the stepparent. Our stepparents loved and cared for us, but they could never replace what was missing in our hearts from the birth parent that was not in the home.

When I started dating, I did as my sisters had done. I would stay after school with some girlfriends to talk with boys because I did not know how to talk about dating to my parents. We never had these types of conversations. I would skip afterschool band practice sometimes and spend time talking to a boy who liked me. It never occurred to me to see if I could invite someone over to visit. I did learn one thing from my father while living with him and his new family for a few years. I gave a boy my phone number when I was fourteen, a freshman in high school, and he called the house. My dad answered the phone and I heard him say, "Freda does not get boy phone calls" and he hung up the phone. Then he told me, "You can't have boy phone calls until you are sixteen," and that was one of three comments that I can recall my dad said to me about dating.

I had my first heartbreak when I was in college and it hurt so badly. I never knew something could hurt so deeply. I lost part of my healthy soul in that relationship. He was always cheating and sneaking around to see other women. I became obsessed with looking for signs of him cheating so that I could confront him and catch him in a lie. I just knew I would find something so I kept looking incessantly and I always found what I was looking for. It eventually tore us apart because he was a cheater and I completely distrusted him. I did not have the emotional strength to leave him even though I was so unhappy and knew I could never marry him because I would be completely miserable. The day he broke up with me was the best gift he could have ever given me, though I was heartbroken and hurt for a long time.

A couple of years later, I met a guy who liked me and who had features that reminded me of my ex. We dated and there I was in another committed relationship. After about a year or so, it happened again. I found out he had been sneaking around seeing his former girlfriend. That time I thought I'd lose my mind. Not because I was so in love with him, it was more about how I began to feel about myself and about men for that matter. *Why would he do that*, I thought. My self-esteem had taken a hard blow once again. My trust in men was ruined. It seemed to me that the culture in Chicago when it came to dating always involved people having more than one significant other. This is what I experienced and observed with my family and friends.

I stayed in the relationship though I was unhappy. He claimed he loved me, but I was hurt and my feelings had changed. I was hurting and did not know how to process or overcome what I was experiencing. I thought I would have a nervous breakdown. That is when I saw a counselor for the first time, trying to figure out how to feel better, how to stop feeling so sad. I prayed often, asking God for strength and guidance. One day after Sunday service, I knelt at the altar and told God how much I was hurting and how much I needed his help. I talked with him about how I had not done well choosing a male friend who would be faithful to me. I prayed, "Lord please send me someone who loves you more than he loves me because then I will know he will treat me well and will never cheat on me."

I was twenty-three when I met my former husband and it was not long after I had prayed that prayer. I was emotionally broken from heartaches and the unfaithfulness of men who claimed to love me. I soon learned he too was broken unfaithfulness from past relationships. We were two emotionally broken individuals coming together with unresolved issues from our past.

He was a guest minister at my church on youth Sunday. I walked into the church late and he watched me from the pulpit as I joined the choir just before we were to sing.

I had an inkling he was checking me out so I lingered around the church after service and went back inside to see if he would approach me, and he did. He asked his cousin to introduce us. He gave me his number and asked me to call him that evening. I was always active in the church. I taught Sunday school, directed the choir, and spoke at different events, so a minister being attracted to me was not foreign—if you know what I mean.

We talked by phone late that night, and he was a good talker and talked about himself and his life, and asked me a lot of questions about my life. He said he was looking for a wife so he was trying to learn as much about me as he could. He was home in Chicago visiting his parents for the weekend and was going back south where he was currently living the next day. When he returned home, we talked on the phone for hours every day. We talked a lot about God, the teachings in the scriptures and what true salvation really meant. After about three days of talking on the phone, he said God told him that I was his wife. I responded, "Really? God didn't tell me that." He replied, "He will". I thought, *when did God start speaking to folks like that?* I'd never heard of God telling someone whom they would marry, but he had my attention because of the prayer I had prayed. The timing was right in stride with my prayers to God. I was done with all the craziness and infidelity from men who said they loved me. I did not know then that just because you are Christians, living wholeheartedly for God, serving in the church, and teaching people about God and how to live the Christian life, you are not exempt from having trouble in your marriage.

He asked me how I felt about starting a church. I said that would be good, as I was raised in the church and had been in church all my life. I recalled when I was about nine that I had a vision or premonition to build a church and in my innocence, tried to build one out of some old bricks and sand from a building, I view that childhood experience as a foreshadow of what I'd be called to do as an adult, that had been torn down that were across the ally from our backyard. I soon discovered I could not make the walls stay up, so I ended that project.

I continued to think about my life, my future, my prayers, and my hopes of building a good life and someday having a family. At some point I believed what he was telling me, that it was God's will for us to marry. I believed he was the answer to my prayers. I felt some type of internal confirmation that God had brought us together, something like a strong intuition, an inner knowing that you just can't ignore. After his many visits to Chicago, our families met, and after three months of dating, we got married. I resigned from the Social Security Administration, packed up my belongings, and moved from my mother's house to the South. One week later we started a church. I was unemployed, and my husband was soon laid off from his job at the state. He received unemployment, and his parents sent us money a few times to help us as we were starting our lives together. After about six months I received a job as a software developer and we received a little support from the church.

Hubby was the pastor and I was the first lady. We had nine members when we started the church in a friend's home. I was immediately in gear as the administrator—my natural gift of getting things organized. Around our second year or so of marriage, hubby went off to seminary for two years in another state and I was soon there after ordained and appointed as co-pastor by our pastor from another church and city, and another minister who lived in our city. My husband flew home once sometimes twice a month. I watched over the church, taught bible studies on Wednesdays, preached on most Sunday mornings and met with members after work in the evenings as needed. I did not want all that responsibility on me alone, but I did it to prevent another minister, who was initially an assistant standing in for a lot of the preaching, from taking over the church. The church continued to grow with 400 to 500, maybe more, in regular attendance at Sunday services. That was a tough season for me. I had never imagined as a new wife I'd be living in a separate state from my husband, but there I was working full-time as a software developer, paying all the bills at home, and overseeing the church.

After two years I told my husband he needed to come home. I struggled with the advances of our friend who was a minister. He was pursuing me hard while my husband was away. He'd stop by often indicating he was checking on me to make sure everything was ok. He was the only person I could really tell how unhappy I was over the years and how I was questioning so much about what was happening in our lives as the ministry continued to grow. I told my husband if he did not come home I did not think I could remain faithful. I informed him that our friend was telling me I better watch out because one of the ladies at the church was really liking my husband implying something was going on between them. I had been questioning him about this young lady and their interactions, him going over to her apartment during some of his visits home and becoming so friendly with her. He became angry and responded this was only being said because our friend was trying to get in my panties.

Eventually, he came home, transferred schools and completed his last year of seminary in our city. My husband was back and in full swing and I could get some relief. A few years later because of our continued growth, I resigned from my secular job, and began working at the church full time. In due course I was managing twenty or more full-time staff at the church, a multi-million dollar budget, preaching and teaching classes, running a second nonprofit we started, serving as superintendent of the Christian school we opened, co-hosting a Christian television broadcast, and raising five children, our three and my niece and nephew. We had a lot of support staff with the children and the kids went to the church school we had started, so they'd be in my office after school and at the church with us. My schedule was mine, so I was able to manage our lives quite comfortably. I loved it.

At some point my husband started disliking me being over the business aspect of the ministries we had started together. We were aware of many other pastoral couples across the country who, were having similar problems in their marriages. Some men for different reasons were having problems with their wives having so much influence in the church. He no longer liked the staff reporting to me, though I had been running the business aspect of the ministries for years. He had been content with vision casting, planning, holding meetings, and preaching/teaching. But he decided he wanted complete authority and control over everything. He felt I had too much influence with the staff and the members and he wanted that to change. He decided he wanted the staff reporting to him. He also decided I should not be honored at our annual Founder's Week celebrations, a celebration we shared from the inception of the ministry. It was a weeklong event that had been occurring for years. We invited guest speakers from across the country and guest psalmists and it culminated with an elaborate black-tie affair hosted at one of the local hotels. He decided that only he would be honored, because he wanted all the honor and adoration of our church family and wanted my role and influence diminished, and that is exactly what happened. I made no public objections and mentioned to no one but him that I did not agree.

He was separating me from the staff and changing many of the church members' view of me and my role in the church. He wanted it to be said that he had built the ministry without me. Surely, he was the pastor when we started the church, but we did start that ministry together. I asked how he could do that to me, reminding him how I had walked away from my career and poured my life into working in the Lord's house. He minimized all that I had done, including overseeing the ministry as it continued to grow, serving and encouraging the members as their co-pastor, and paying all the bills at home for over two years while he was away in seminary.

He had the audacity to say that since I was the one living in the apartment at home every day I should have paid all the bills—not him. He conveniently ignored the fact that he too called the apartment home. He chose not to acknowledge the sacrifices that I made when I left my mother's home and all my family and friends in Chicago, and walked away from my career with the government because I had pledged my life to him, to live with him in a state I had never visited before I knew him. He disregarded the fact that I was "holding it down" on the home front and building up God's people in prayer and in the word as God continued to bring in more and more souls while he was hundreds of miles away. Adding insult to injury, he would tell me that what I did, was doing, and had done over the years was no big deal and that anyone could have done it. I guess he wanted me to know that he felt I was insignificant and had no value in the ministry in his eyes. It was a dagger in my heart; part of me died that day.

In response to that painful disregard, and trying to fight back because I was so hurt, I responded in kind with,

"Anyone could have done what you've done because God could have chosen someone else to lead his people, but he chose us together. God chooses whom he chooses. We do not get to tell God what to do. I told him we were both vessels being used by God, utilizing our gifts in obedience to him. I was stating what I believed to be the truth. God can raise up anyone to do anything, and he was no exception." He was infuriated and said that he could never be replaced; he was irreplaceable.

I recall hearing him chatting with his friend once, talking about removing me from my position. His friend said, "How are you going to do that? That's Pastor Freda," and it was said so that I could hear. With all the disregard I never saw him quite the same. I was convinced that he did not love me; he loved himself. I found my purpose in working with God's people and using my gifts that God had allowed to flourish. I was crushed to the core. As one minister told me, he wanted me to be his cheerleader on the sideline saying, "Look at all that you have done."

Some of the members shared with me that he'd been telling some of the church folks, I guess you'd call them the inner circle that he was unhappy with me and he was sharing things about me that he disliked to groups of people. I was told he was purposefully tainting their view of me and painting a picture of himself as the mistreated husband whose wife was not loving and not taking care of him. He would openly say things like black men chose women of other races because black women were too strong and did not know how to submit. He would say it in small groups and even across the pulpit. Of course, the majority of the women at the church were African American, so when he would make statements like that we'd just look and say nada. It was my strength that helped us build and grow. What was once view as a great asset was being view as a negative character trait.

I don't think he ever understood that when you do and say things to people, not just me but also anyone, that wounds them deeply, it changes the nature of the relationship. And if you continue with those types of actions, the damage to the relationship is often irreparable and the relationship can be permanently severed. He never did understand that! Perhaps he never will. Saying what you want in the church regardless to how it appeared or whether it hurt someone or not because you are the pastor is unwise.

He'd preach on how the women should conduct themselves in a marriage—nothing wrong with that, but talking about things that he felt were wrong in our marriage without mentioning our names did not feel good. I did not need a sermon. We needed counseling, an unbiased third party. I imagine he thought he was actually helping us, I suppose. What else would make someone do that? It had the opposite effect. This drove me further away. By nature he was a fusser and would explode when he got upset because something did not go the way he wanted. If something was unacceptable, was not done correctly, or went wrong during a service, you would be openly rebuked in meetings and given a good lip lashing in front of everyone in the room. Maybe he thought verbal lashings would motivate someone—nope, not true for me and not true for most people.

I needed love, appreciation, compassion, nurture, privacy, and understanding. We needed skilled professional help that we would both submit to wholeheartedly. Having a few talks and thinking all would be well was a fantasy that would never cure anything. We went through the motions of counseling once and he rebuked the counselor for making little of me being late a lot. I mean he went off saying how this was an issue in the black community and how dare he say being late was not that bad. I just thought to myself, *oh well I guess this guy won't be helping us*, and that was the end of that.

With members over the house all the time, literally every day, he'd often, teach in these small intimate settings, both men and women, on sex in a marriage and how to keep things interesting. I was so messed up inside and took everything so personally because I knew that was not going on in our marriage. Everyone would look at me and of course I always had to have on my game face and pretend to not be fazed. It takes a lot of energy to focus on acting how you think people think you should act. I became masterful at pretending not to be fazed by things.

With all the different emotions bottled up inside, life became rather lonely. I could be in a room full of people and feel so lonely, because I was emotionally close to no one.

No counseling was allowed for me because we were so well known in the city and he feared our business would get out. It made sense to me, and I did not want that. He was not a proponent of professional counseling, at least not for our family. This is often true in some cultures so people often suffer in silence. I had no close girlfriends or family members that I could bare my soul to for some real support because I feared what people would say and think, and besides, it was not appropriate for me to bare my heart to the members because of the nature of the relationship (pastor and member is sort of like counselor and counselee). I also did not want to hinder anyone's relationship with God by telling them all my problems. This included my family. Holding in my thoughts and feelings and allowing what I perceived others thought I should or should not do or say to control my behavior and actions was also contributing to my discontent.

Early in our marriage my husband had an early onset of diabetes and over the years he developed problems with his feet after standing for long periods, so he liked to have foot rubs and wanted me to be okay with some of the women from the church rubbing and massaging his feet while we sat around and fellowshipped with people from the church. I hated that. I felt so violated. I would say, "Let's get a professional." I told him the men could help him with his feet, or one of the women whom I knew was not particularly interested in men, or my younger sister because they both were pretty good at giving massages and did not mind. He did not understand the problem. I told him none of the male elders or ministers would be having women massage their feet because their wives would not like it. He was an open person, and spoke openly about many things. I on the other hand, am a private person when it comes to personal matters and if you want your feet rubbed because they hurt, that could happen when we were alone and not in a room full of people while we are sitting round talking. It was just weird to me.

And then there is the God factor. What is God saying, and what does God want from me? When you pour your heart out to God, trying with everything within you to be yielded to his will and his teachings in the bible, you can get confused about what is God's will and what is man's will. What a thin line to discern between. Is the pastor speaking on behalf of God or is he speaking out of his flesh and speaking his own biases? I was afraid that I would go to hell if I ever left, or I'd be lost and out of God's will forever. I often prayed, "Lord, please let me never walk away from you." Of course God does not abandon us, but we can choose to walk away from him. I was not emotionally healthy and did not know how to get better.

I almost completely withdrew emotionally and physically from the marriage for so many reasons. Sadly at some point I felt uncomfortable being with him intimately. I became more and more intimidated, and insecure in my marriage. It was pretty obvious that some of the women in the church liked the pastor, and they'd constantly stroke his ego and prance around like a bunch of floozies wanting me out of the way so that they could take my place. We were emotionally detached and were growing further apart. I felt I was in competition with the other women who were strutting around the church and following him everywhere he went. I refused to compete. I hated the thought of it and it was beneath me. Even if I had the mind to compete, because I was so insecure, I was afraid he'd like them better and I would not be able to bear it. My insecurities were resurfacing.

I now know that a lot of my responses and the way I internalized things were due to me being depressed. I had been depressing so many emotions for so many years. I did not know this then. I found this out sometime later, after the divorce when I finally got professional counseling to help me make sense of things.

I was no virgin when we married so I knew how to love both emotionally and physically (with room for growth, of course). The problems, the hurt, the scolding, and lip lashings took away the desire. I was unable to be what a man desires and needs from his woman. I was paralyzed. He was unable to see the depths of my pain and hurt, or he just did not care. He was no longer the man I wanted and needed. We were both unhappy. What generally happens when people are so unhappy for so long is either one or both will step out on the marriage. For men it is generally a physical thing and for women it's often an emotional need that may turn physical just because of the emotional bond that forms. Though sometimes it can be different. That would be the 80/20 rule—80% of the time this would be true.

Eventually he said God never told him to marry me. People have to be careful about what they say God told them, or should I say we should take pause when people say God told them thus and so, even if they are convincing. Well, I guess he made it up or became confused as he looked back over the past eleven years and wanted out of the marriage. It's amazing what we'll tell ourselves so we can do what we want to do and have what we want. I was not confused. I knew what we had discussed and how often we had told the story for years while we still liked each other. We were brought together, and we decided we were unhappy and agreed to get a divorce. God can put you together, but it is up to you to maintain and do the work to keep the marriage healthy. He had the church history rewritten and my name omitted. I don't imagine I was ever put back in the historical records. I'm glad God is the one who gives out the rewards.

How did such great intentions and sincere love for the things of God and His kingdom get so off track? I will say, as the scripture says, it is "The lust of the flesh, the lust of the eyes and the pride of life" coupled with other developmental issues we both encountered during our childhood and dating years. We needed help but were so far gone we did not want to recover. We lost our focus and never regained clear vision for our union.

As the ministry grew, our relationship grew further and further apart. We rarely spent time with just the two of us or us and the children. People were with us all the time. He seemed to need people around all the time so that meant no *us* but us and them, literally. He was fun to be around and knew how to have a good time, and I enjoyed hanging out and having people over and having fun as well. However, a woman needs her man to herself sometimes and she needs to feel that she is always number one and that everyone else falls somewhere else in the line. It was like that in the beginning.

Material gifts can only do so much and will never replace intimacy. That is fundamental to any healthy relationship. Surely, pastors must be given to hospitality, and we both had that covered, but the marriage piece got lost somewhere in the shuffle.

Since we spent most of our time with people at the church, I was just one among many, everyone at the senior pastor's feet (no pun intended), so to speak. I no longer felt special. We were disconnected relationally, and I did not feel romantic or sexy with him, as a wife should after awhile. We were great ministry partners and I was the mother of his children. We did love each other but it surely did not feel like it a lot of the time.

I remember once one of the ladies at the church asked me a question saying, "Pastor Freda, why is it that a woman who knows what to do in a marriage does not do it?" She was asking me this because she was one of those my husband had been venting to. I responded, "When you have been so hurt emotionally, sometimes you are not capable of opening yourself up to that person emotionally or intimately anymore. The wounds are too deep, and it is not safe." She just looked at me.

I felt that he could throw me away and I wanted a relationship, a man and all that comes with a healthy loving relationship, and family time that did not include everyone else. I wanted us to like spending time with each other. We had it in the beginning, but we were so busy, it was lost in all the ministry building. I eventually learned that this is so typical of many pastors with their families, and nothing unique to us. Though not true for all pastors. Some are wiser than we were.

Many pastors fail to accept that they are married to their spouses and not to a church. Jesus is married to the church, as the church is the Bride of Christ (Revelations 1:7-9, II Corinthians 11:2), not the bride of the pastor. The church and God are not one and the same. But some pastors will argue against this all in the name of doing God's work. Putting your service in the church before your family is no different than the snare many professionals fall into as they build secular careers. It mirrors the unbalanced actions of many ambitious CEOs, politicians, lawyers laboring to make partner, or medical doctors building a thriving practice. The only difference is the pastorate is a sacred call carried out under the umbrella of the church. The snare and youthful ambitions are often the same or very similar when the relationship with the spouse and children are not natured adequately.

It's a call, not a profession or career, they will argue. In the grand scheme of things, the result (of focusing on one thing to an extreme and ignoring another) will be the same. If you don't nurture, put in the time, do the hard work, seek professional help, or do whatever it takes in a marriage and family, someone is going to be unhappy, and disaster on some level is inevitable. I don't know if pastors, men and women, are just self-deceived and just too full of themselves to see this truth, or if they just ignore the truth. Do they just want what they want, how they want it, and the failed marriages and confused children are just par for the course? This is the reason for some of the affairs in these marriages, and the harm suffered by the children and God is not pleased with us.

I had been unhappy for a long time and I guess he was too, just for different reasons. Somewhere along the way God stopped being the focus, and success, status, personal desires and pride among other things became the blinders. The things he once love about me like my reasoning and analytical abilities, my leadership skills and my confidence which were vital as we were building he began to despise. If I did not agree, he felt I was not submissive. I was just saying what I felt or how I viewed things. My thoughts are my thoughts and no one thinks exactly the same and to have a different opinion is not a sin. However if I'd disagree strongly, I'd be accused of not being submissive. No matter how hard I tried,

I just could not change enough. So, I decided: "You can never change enough to be what someone else wants. As soon as you think you've figured it out, the expectations will change. It will always be a moving target."

Well, one day it all exploded. We decided to divorce. He told me he could have any woman he wanted, and I just needed to get with the program. I thought I could be happy with some wonderful man who would love me for who I was. I believed he was cheating with some of the women in the church. He thought I was cheating. It was a mess.

I agreed that we would tell the church that I no longer wanted that life. I thought that would be the best thing for the members and it would keep God's church intact. Boy was I mistaken. It turned out that everyone was being told that I had an affair and the marriage was over. Many pastors were called, and I was slandered and labeled as the adulteress. I was devastated, truly crushed. Everyone was looking at me like I had the scarlet letter carved in my forehead. I was told not to come to the church anymore because he was ready to live the single life and be free to date. Why would he tell others this about me? So that he could say he had scriptural grounds to get divorced. Again there was no regard for how that would make me look or feel. I did not retaliate. Many negative things about the pastor during and after our marriage came out through the mouths of others over the years.

The church family (members) was hurt as they loved both of us and they did not want us to divorce. They wanted us to work it out. Eventually I was informed that the members were told not to contact me, and so they didn't. I was pretty much thrown away. I could not believe the people who had been close to me, eaten in my home, helped care for my children, did not reach out to me to see how I was doing, not even the couple who allowed us to start the church in their home. The members were told I was no longer their pastor. When they saw me, they would speak but that was it. Three people out of all those members, probably over a thousand dialed my number to check on me. They were kind to me and helped me in the darkest season of my life. They said that they refused to be told how they should relate to me. Each of them, two women and one man, truly cared about how I was doing. They were used by God to be there for me, each in distinct ways.

God gave me favor with a few pastors because they knew us and they knew things did not add up. I was nurtured in their homes and their churches and via phone conversations for a few years, as I worked through all my pain and confusion, and as I questioned my beliefs and all the teachings I had been under for years. I was basically at square one. The only thing that I was truly certain of was "There is a God." How he expressed himself to us, worked through his ministers, and the intricate details of the scriptures were all up for grabs. I had to rediscover God and his teachings on my own and decide what I believed. I cried out to God many nights in prayer seeking to relieve my pain, desperately seeking to make sense of my present and future state in life and the Body of Christ. It took years before I could be deeply involved in a church. I tried once, but the pain was so raw I had to eventually leave that church. I remained faithful in prayer, reading the word of God and church attendance at another church and allowed myself to receive the word and heal.

I was in a bad place. I found a counselor and was diagnosed with clinical depression. I was reassured that having independent thoughts was a normal human behavior and had nothing to do with being submissive. It's amazing how something so simple can become questionable when you are not able to process properly. For quite a while I ached and cried and felt so lost. I wondered if I had made the right decision. I was concerned about being in God's perfect will and I was sad for my children and how they would be impacted. My therapist helped me understand the importance of talking about how I felt. I was depressed because I had suppressed so many of my true feelings. I have the right to disagree and speak up for myself and talk about how things affected me. The more I talked the more I understood why I was so sad. I wanted to know with all certainty that God and I were okay. I was afraid that God was not pleased with me because I could not survive in the marriage and just did not want to live the life we were living. It was not good for me. I truly believe if I had stayed and things remained the same I may have suffered a severe breakdown.

I've learned to speak my truth and require mutual respect from anyone I am to be in a relationship with, platonic or romantic. That is a commitment I made to myself. I understand grace in a way I never knew it before my divorce. I learned to set boundaries in my relationships and not allow anyone to control me, or demand that I be someone I am not. I also learned that someone can speak and teach things that are true, but if it is delivered harshly or condemning, the truth can sound like a lie and be rejected because of the delivery. The bible teaches about speaking the truth in love so that we may grow to become the mature Body of Christ…(Ephesians 4:15). I worked on my self-confidence and self-esteem and the negative self-talk that kept me in fear. I worked through depression and remained in therapy until I was better and able to truly move on with my life.

It was a difficult journey, but I am truly a better person on the other side of that life lesson. While I was healing, I reestablished my career in corporate America, made new friends, and began traveling. I felt free, all the heaviness was lifted, and I was enjoying my new life. I bought a Mercedes Benz for me, and a Cadillac Escalade for the kids and me. I was living my best life. Initially I told myself that I did not need a man. After all, I had money and wasn't lacking financially. I had children, and I could take care of them and me; so I thought I did not need a man. Eventually I rethought that and decided that I do like romantic intimacy and was open to dating.

I dated and made some mistakes or as they say kissed a few frogs along the way. However, when I realized a relationship was not going to work for me, it was not what I needed or wanted, I called it quits. I had set some standards and I knew what I needed and wanted, and I knew what I did not need and did not want in a relationship. I kept it real, always open and honest, and kept it moving when it was time to move on. It was not easy, but it was necessary.

About five years after my divorce, I met my prince charming. He is my compatible love match, my soul's suitable complement. What an awesome, intelligent, caring soul. We complement each other on so many levels. He loves my confidence and my strength as a person and encourages me to pursue whatever dreams or aspirations I have. We like each other and we love each other and we are in love. My husband says he has never talked so much in all his life. Open communication and expressing how we feel is a vital part of our marriage. Raphael and I have been married for fifteen years.

Raphael supported and encouraged my decision to attended seminary full time to study theology, refine my belief in God and the local church and be further equipped in ministry to teach God's word and serve people from all walks of life. I learned a lot and solidified my position on many biblical topics. I was also trained in community ministry, missions, and pastoral care, and was certified as a premarital and marriage counselor.

I was able to move on with my life after what felt like a mountain of pain and confusion. It took dedication and determination, and seeking and receiving help, and eventually I found my way, and this is why I wrote this book to help you in your journey. To let you know that you, too, can heal, rebuild and move on healthier, happier, and more fulfilled.

Through HELP Enterprises, I continue to work with numerous individuals who are struggling to make sense of their lives after their marriages have ended in divorce. I support them through healing, rebuilding, and moving on with their lives and being open to finding true love.

In the following chapters I share some approaches I've used to help others as they transitioned through the disappointment of divorce and failed relationships. Take the journey to healing with me. Let me guide you through a successful strategy that I know can work if you are ready to make the commitment to move on with me by your side.

Chapter 3

THE ROAD MAP TO A HEALTHY, HAPPY AND FULFILLING LIFE

T he following is an outline of your journey to a healthy, happy, and more fulfilling life.

I provide a brief summary of what will be discussed in each chapter. While I believe each chapter is vitally important and should be read, you can read the chapters in any order based on what jumps out at you and still apply the strategies. Chapter 5 and Chapter 7 work together, they provide balance as you do the healing work. It is important not to skip Chapter 7 after you have read Chapter 5.

Within these chapters I share some approaches I've used to successfully move on after a painful divorce and how I have helped others as they transitioned through the disappointment of failed relationships and marriages. Take the journey with me. Let me guide you through a successful strategy that I know can work if you are ready to move on with me by your side.

Chapter 4: Getting the Help I Need

In chapter 4 I strongly emphasize the importance of caring for yourself and having the courage to seek help from people you know and various resources that provide positive support for individuals going through divorce. You will learn to put yourself first so that you can get the help you need. I provide different resources you can find in your city that are available for you while you heal and rebuild your new life.

Chapter 5: Good Grief, I Wasn't Prepared for This

Chapter 5 gives details about how grieving a failed marriage or relationship will feel. I discuss what grief is and the harm you do to yourself if you ignore your emotions and try to live as though you are not impacted by the loss of the marriage. You will learn about the different emotional phases experienced during and after divorce, and how to cope in each phase. You'll learn why grief is necessary for healing, how to acknowledge your grief, how to work through the loss of your marriage, and know when you are nearing the end of the grief process.

Chapter 6: A Time to Forgive

In Chapter 6 I discuss why forgiving someone is healthy for you and why refusing to forgive keeps you connected to the event and the offender. You'll learn common misconceptions about what it means to forgive and why forgiving is essential to healthy emotional healing. You will also learn how to forgive yourself and how to forgive others who you believe do not deserve to be forgiven.

Chapter 7: Becoming the Best Me

In Chapter 7, I discuss the importance of balancing your grief work with positive affirmations about yourself. You will learn how to build a healthy relationship with yourself and develop healthy routines for removing negative thoughts and replacing them with positive thinking that is vital to feeling good and enjoying life.

Chapter 8: What's Best for the Children?

Chapter 8 gives you examples for how to best relate with your children based on their emotional needs at different ages in the development process. You will learn how to protect your children from some of the negative things you may be experiencing and what is and is not appropriate to share with the children. You'll also learn strategies to make things easier for the children during and after the divorce.

Chapter 9: Building Healthy Relationships

Chapter 9 prepares you for dating and provides suggestions for identifying some of the traits that are very important to you when choosing to date. You'll learn about not compromising qualities in a relationship that are true needs and not just wants. You'll learn strategies for choosing wisely when you are ready to date and remaining true to your personal values and belief. You will also learn the importance of establishing boundaries in new relationships and when it's time to call it quits and move on.

Chapter 10: My Spiritual Life

Chapter 10 focuses on being clear about your relationship with God and learning to embrace God's unconditional love. You'll learn what the bible says about divorce, and how to heal and grow when wounded spiritually by church leaders and members of your church community.

Chapter 11: When the Healing Gets Tough

Chapter 11 focuses on the obstacles you may encounter as you are implementing the methods outlined for healing during and after divorce. You'll receive reinforcement for remaining consistent and not giving up when things get difficult or you become discouraged as you are doing the hard work for healthy emotional healing and positive rebuilding for your new life.

Chapter 12: I'm Moving On

At the end of the book, I provide a short story about a client who has navigated through the healing process and is enjoying her dating life as a single woman. I emphasize the importance of not giving up and continuing your journey to more happiness, healing and fulfillment. You receive a high-level summary of everything you've learned and the importance of using this book as a road map to be referenced often as you heal and rebuild your life. I encourage you to remain true to yourself as you to continue the work you have started so that you can reap the benefits.

As you work through the 8-step method for *Healing The Wounds Of Divorce* you must be patient and not expect things to change or be over after a few weeks. Grief cannot be put on a timetable. You process it as you experience it. But you must stay the course and continue to do the work. Some days you may feel no particular way, other days you may not want to leave the house. Be sure to write it all down and evaluate what you are feeling. Read over what you have written in the past weeks or months and compare it to how you are feeling presently. This will help you gauge how you are progressing through your emotions and the grief phases.

Chapter 4

TAKING CARE OF YOURSELF

S ometimes admitting you need help can be one of the biggest challenges you face in getting on the road to healing and wholeness. Some people view getting help as a sign of weakness, of not being in control of their well-being, or they feel embarrassed or awkward. No matter what emotions you may feel, know this—you are not the first person to feel this way, and you surely will not be the last. What is important here is that you have the courage and ability to recognize and admit that you need some help in getting over a tremendous loss in your life. No one should go through a loss or grieve alone. We all need someone to help us along the way at various times in our lives. For some, it is easy to ask for help, but for others it is difficult.

Lynette told me, "I just do not like talking to strangers. I feel so odd and I just do not like the idea of sitting in a stranger's office that I know nothing about and pouring out my soul. I'd rather talk to someone I know. This makes me more comfortable." She went for years with mild to moderate depression because she was unwilling to get the medical attention that would help her feel better. Since I know Lynette, and I am familiar with the signs of depression and anxiety, I knew she was depressed and urged her to see a psychiatrist. After a few years, she eventually told her primary care doctor how she was feeling, and he confirmed that she was depressed and prescribed her some medication to help her cope and feel better.

Although she eventually got some medical attention, she has not been able to heal and recover from all the tragedies she has experienced because she is still not doing the inner work that is needed. She must be willing to work with someone to assist her in identifying the problems. Then she will be able to address them, and. a plan can be developed to help her work through the painful emotions.

It hurts me to see people suffer. And it hurts even more when I know how to help someone, but they are unwilling to receive the help or do the work that is needed to get better. My hope for you is that you will be open to trying new things so that you can become a better you—a healthy you—a happy you. If you are willing to put aside any hindrances and make a decision to do any and everything you can to get better, you will get better, but the decision to begin healing must begin with you. You must resolve within yourself that you are not willing to ignore how you feel or remain sad, confused, lost, apathetic, depressed, or angry. Tell yourself that you will get better by any means necessary, and mean it. Once you make that resolution, you are truly on your way and can get the best support and results available.

The first thing I'd like you to do is identify at least two people who you fully trust who you can talk with freely and openly. If you are not able to identify anyone, that is okay. The next thing to do is to look for a support group for individuals going through a divorce or an online divorce program that is provided virtually. Doing either is good, but at least one is necessary for individual support. Having someone or a group to identify with and talk with about how you are feeling and getting emotional support is part of your mental and emotional healing journey. You should know that your feelings are not unusual. Others have similar feelings as you do when working through divorce. Venting allows you to relieve tension and emotional pain. It stops you from bottling up your feelings hoping they will go away.

Divorce coaching is another resource that can be helpful and supportive. Divorce coaching is often offered online, for individuals and in groups and has been helpful for many. These programs generally last for several weeks and provide an opportunity for you to receive support from the comfort of your home using a computer and video conferencing where you are allowed to see the host and others if you are working with a group.

Individual therapy is sometimes necessary after a difficult breakup and it can be quite helpful. If you are ever at a point where you are unable to function or perform your usual routine tasks, unable to go to work, or anything similar, you should look for a professional therapist immediately. Psychology Today at www.psychologytoday.com has a list of licensed professional therapist, psychologist and psychiatrists with their photographs, information about their practice, the types of people they service, whether or not they take insurance, and the fees they charge.

If you have experienced any type of trauma or abuse, in the marriage, in the past or present, Eye Movement Desensitization and Reprocessing (EMDR) is a therapy that is designed to help individuals get through traumatic events much quicker than the traditional types of therapy. This therapy works by focusing on your past, present, and future. Past trauma or recent trauma can prevent you from fully healing because the harm you have endured may be dormant and therefore, you may not be able to heal from the event on your own.

Studies have shown that people who have suffered trauma may react out of that trauma, even if they are not aware of it. A licensed professional EMDR psychologist can help you heal from the emotional distress that is the result of disturbing life experiences.

A good friend, a relative, a divorce support group, a divorce coach, a therapist, a licensed EMDR psychologist, and a psychiatrist are some suggestions of support systems you should put in place to assist you as you heal and move forward. At a minimum, everyone should have one or two friends, preferably two, a divorce support group, or a divorce coach. Take a few minutes to identify the support you believe you need before moving forward. Write down the names of the friends or family members or go online and search "divorce recovery groups" in your city and write down the names of a few places you can check out. Also, search online for some divorce coaches and schedule some time to contact them for more information.

When looking for professional help, be selective. It is common to see a couple of different psychologists/therapists/psychologists before you find the person that is right for you. It is important that you feel a connection with the person you will work with. You should be comfortable working with the therapist you choose.

People from all walks of life seek professional therapy for their mental health needs. Therapists often have a therapist that they see for mental health support so that they can stay healthy and work through their problems. I know many pastors and pastor's wives who have seen and continue to see counselors outside and inside the church. Many do so in secret because it feels safe for them. But I will tell you, when I heard my current pastor, now emeritus, first say over the pulpit that he and his wife had been to marriage counseling three times over the years, I was so proud that he was able to share that part of their lives with our congregation so that the parishioners would know that it is okay to seek professional help and not be ashamed. Our pastor was leading by example.

Chief executive officers, professional athletes, medical doctors, and attorneys use these professionals from time to time. Life events trouble everyone at some point in life. Some people are willing to get the help they need, and others are not. I would rather talk with a professional to see if they can help me rather than suffer alone with no prospects for a solution. I have been helped tremendously through counseling. Once I was free to get help, it was the best thing I could have ever done. I went from feeling like I was carrying an elephant on my back everyday to feeling as light as a feather. I was able to recognize myself again. My counselor was able to support me in making the choices I believed were best for me and helped me work through a lot of painful events in my life.

Over the years I have found that men are generally less likely to receive counseling or therapy. Daryl Goldenberg, PH. D indicates, "For many men, admitting to having a personality flaw (or two or three) can feel like admitting to having leprosy." Men generally state they don't need anyone telling them how to solve their problems. I've learned that this is a defense mechanism, and often a fear of being vulnerable and feeling out of control.

Goldenberg says "Many of the men I've worked with have presented themselves as hardheaded negotiators (treating their marriage like a business deal). They resisted taking action until they were threatened with foreclosure–the marriage ending. At that point, there was a flurry of activity, pleadings for a second chance, or even accepting the ominous choice of therapy. For many of these men, it was only once they faced this life startling event like a spouse's ultimatum, that they felt forced into a deeper emotional reality."

I have also learned over the years that certain cultural groups look at professional counseling negatively and discourage family and friends from seeking support from these medical or licensed professionals. The view that has developed for some is "only crazy people" go to counseling and take medication for mental and emotional problems. Fear of the unknown or buy-in to stigmas and biases, or even potential shame prevent many people from getting the help they need. They may suffer for years when they could have received a therapeutic intervention and proper support for an undiagnosed illness.

I encourage you not to let your religious, cultural or familial biases dictate the type of help you get for yourself. I know this can be hard because I experienced this myself. At times people feel if you have faith, then just pray and trust God. Praying and trusting God is good and a practice to encourage, but we must also remember that all knowledge belongs to God and God has allowed humanity to tap into His knowledge and wisdom to discover and develop therapies, herbs, and medicines that are available to us for our benefit and well being

Mental illness should be viewed like any other illness. If a person has symptoms associated with diabetes, high blood pressure, or cancer, any reasonable person will tell them to go to the doctor or an emergency room to receive medical attention to get well. The same should be true for anyone suffering mentally or emotionally. Women and men alike have dedicated their lives to understanding the human mind and the evolving moods and behaviors. This is done to understand the mental imbalances that inhibit an individual from engaging in life sustaining activities. Anyone who would speak against someone seeking professional counseling when they are suffering mentally or emotionally is not wise, and is ignorant of the advancements in the mental health profession and the benefits that millions continue to receive.

If anyone tells you that you don't need to see a professional counselor, do what you know is best for you. Sometimes you need more than prayer, you need help from our healing communities of professionals.

If you are seeking professional counseling, you should ensure that the counselor is licensed. There are excellent options secular and Christian, who you choose will depend on your personal needs. I know of a few pastors who absolutely, under no circumstances, wanted a Christian counselor. They wanted a professional who was not a Christian because it was the church that was causing all of their anguish, so having someone outside of the church who is licensed and highly educated in the mental health arena would provide an unbiased view of what they were experiencing. Each of them are still serving in the Christian church and thriving in their ministries.

I personally prefer a professional licensed psychologist who has a Christian background. What matters to me is that they understand my beliefs, so that they are aware of how I see the world and what is vitally important to me. I have also gotten advice and support from pastors both male and female, but this support was more directional and not long-term. I like to speak with the leaders in my church, where I feel safe and where we share the same beliefs and values. In the past, I was not able to do this because of certain biases that existed. I felt they could not help me because of where they were in their lives.

I cannot stress enough the importance of having a friend or family member you can trust and with whom you feel emotionally safe. This is so important! You don't need judgment from anyone right now. You need support and understanding. Now that does not mean some of your thoughts or feelings are not way out in left field. I am saying you need someone who understands how you feel and what you are going through, even if they don't agree with you.

"The friend who can be silent with us in a moment of despair or confusion, who can stay with us in an hour of grief and bereavement, who can tolerate not knowing... not healing, not curing... that is a friend who cares."
– Henri Nouwen

For example, you may feel so angry that you want to bust all the windows out of your ex's car. No one should be singing the popular R&B song "I bust the windows out ya car." That's not recommended and could cause someone to get hurt, put the children in danger, or you could be viewed as an unfit parent or even put in jail. A wise friend may understand how you feel and why you feel that way, but they would not recommend that you do that. It's important to identify a friend with a good sense of judgment.

Self-help and self-care are your closest allies during and after a difficult breakup or divorce. Whether you wanted the divorce or not, you have suffered a significant loss. And with any loss there is hurt and pain and a host of other emotions. We will discuss the various emotions people generally experience during and after a breakup or divorce in Chapter 5.

You may feel as though you don't need to talk with anyone and everything will be fine. Taking that approach is doing you a great injustice. Holding things in is not the same as getting how you feel out in the open. Having some honest conversations about what you have experienced is wise and healthy. You will grow as a person, be less likely to make the same mistakes, and you will be better equipped in future relationships.

Being the best (you) you can be has so much to do with you reaching out to others and learning from the experience with your ex. Why did you choose him? Why did he or you fall out of love? Why did you clash so much? What you need to be most interested in is what you can do about you so that your future is better, and you don't repeat the same mistakes going forward. The only thing you can fix or improve is you. You cannot fix others, nor should you try. Discovering things about yourself and how to be healthy has nothing to do with your ex, but it has everything to do with you, and if applicable, your children.

Utilizing outside resources, counselors, psychologists, psychiatrists, pastors, ministers, friends, relatives, a divorce coach or a support groups is a positive way of getting the support and help that you may need. As you will read in Chapter 5, you will be able to access your mood and determine if you may need professional help.

What to Expect When You Reach out for Help

If you join a professional support group, you will interact with a group of individuals going through similar challenges. Everyone generally introduces themselves and may share a little about their situations. You can share as little or as much as you desire. If you go to see a therapist, you will meet with an individual and they will ask you questions about yourself.

They will share a little about themselves. They may ask you if you have a goal or what you'd like to accomplish. A divorce coach will have strategies that you can implement and work through to help you deal with the difficulties you are experiencing and provide empowering strategies to support in confidence building. A psychiatrist will be helpful if you need medication to get you through some of the rougher times, like depression. Talking with a friend will allow you the freedom to talk and have some accountability as you heal. I would suggest not seeking out a romantic relationship immediately. Your keen senses may not be as vibrant and aware of certain red flags because you are vulnerable. When you are vulnerable you may choose whatever you can get to make yourself feel better. In the end, it may backfire and make things in your life more complicated. I have a general rule when I'm not feeling emotionally well. I do not make any major decisions or big changes in my life because I'm not at my best. This could be relating to anything like making a major purchase, changing jobs, or anything that could be life altering. I do this because I want to be sure I am making a decision that has been thought about and evaluated, and not one based on impulse or out of emotions so that I don't regret my decision later.

Going through a divorce or breakup with someone who you thought you'd spend the rest of your life with is a huge, life-changing event. So many things in your life will change because of this that you never thought about initially. You will have more alone time than you had. If you are an introvert, someone who replenishes themselves or recharges when you're by yourself, this may sound like a good thing initially. However, eventually you will feel his absence. If you are an extrovert, someone who gets energy from being around others, you will feel being alone more intensely when you are at home. Either way, when you are home it will feel different.

When I divorced I had a large lounge chair the type that you can sit in and your entire body can stretch out as you are sitting up. I slept in that oversized lounge chair for months. I could not bring myself to sleep in the bedroom. I felt more secure being in the chair in the family room than in my bedroom. It was a huge adjustment getting used to it just being me and knowing no one would be coming through the door at any point to break the silence or emptiness I felt in the home. I would have never imagined I'd have that type of reaction, but I did.

I became creative when the kids went to their dad's for the weekends. I started inviting people over from work or going to the bookstore to look around and read some good material. I had no family in town, so some days when I could find no one to talk with or be with, I'd just get in the car and drive. It's something how your mind will just think and think and think when you are alone. Eventually I began to enjoy the long drives because I had time to think about my life and reflect. Sometimes I'd have to pull over and stop because I'd find myself crying for extended periods of time, and feeling sorry for myself. The good thing was that I did have my sister, who lived about fifteen hours away by car, who I could call when I needed someone to just be on the other side of the phone. It did not matter what we talked about, just knowing she was there and that she loved me helped me on numerous days. I started taking more frequent trips home to visit my family. I'd go every other month for the weekend, just to have someone close to me who loved me unconditionally. If you remember, I lost my entire community of friends when my ex and I decided to divorce. I no longer had visitors or received phone calls.

One day, I'm not sure how it happened, one of the ladies from the church (one of the three I mentioned earlier) called me and we talked, and we began to hang out and do things together. I could actually talk with her about the marriage and the divorce and she understood. She was well aware of all the craziness that was going on much of which she disliked herself and she eventually left the church. She loved us both and decided that she would not be forced to end her relationship with me.

I became close with another female who I had known through being in ministry. I traveled to conferences with her when I was able to get off work. We became very close and shared some meaningful times. She understood what I was going through and opened her heart and life to me and let me heal. I was hurting and felt so disoriented about my life, and I remember she would tell me to stop, saying, "I am so confused." I needed that. I needed to remove that negative self-talk and replace it with positive affirmations.

She was there for me when my mother died. She jumped on a plane and came to be with me. You learn a lot about people when you are in the midst of life's trials. Those you would expect to be there sometimes are nowhere to be found and those you don't expect to be there show up in ways you never imagined.

Having someone to talk to and spend time with is a huge benefit. When you are feeling sorry for yourself and down in the dumps you can think about those individuals and remind yourself that someone cares and that some good things are happening despite your crappy feelings.

Remember, you are someone special! God our creator fearfully and wonderfully made you (Psalms 139:13-14), and that overrides all negative thoughts about yourself. You are just experiencing a season of life that requires some tender, loving care. You'll need some positive reinforcement, someone to make you laugh and smile, someone to make you leave the house and go for a walk or a drive. We are not made to live our lives in isolation, but rather in community. We live in community and provide support to one another when it is needed. You may need help in this season of your life, but someone else will benefit from leaning on you in the future when they are facing difficult life challenges.

Chapter 5

GOOD GRIEF, I WASN'T PREPARED FOR THIS

"I wasn't prepared for the fact that grief is so unpredictable. It wasn't just sadness, and it wasn't linear. Somehow I'd thought that the first days would be the worst and then it would get steadily better—like getting over the flu. That's not how it was."

– Meghan O'Rourke

What is grief? Grief is the normal process of reacting to a loss and it can be an overwhelming experience. It may seem counter-intuitive to think that the road to healing during and after a failed marriage would involve facing and accepting the pain that has come into your life. Well my friend, this is exactly what I am telling you. Grief is a normal process that we experience when we lose someone who has been an intimate part of our lives. It has many facets and at times the experience with grief can be overwhelming and almost unbearable. Grief is the body's way of expressing how you feel when a major change or loss has occurred.

When a couple divorces, they experience the death of so many things. Many have said going through a divorce is worse than grieving the death of a loved one. We expect everyone to die, and once they are gone, we know that we are no longer able to call or visit with them. Any unresolved issues must be dealt with without the input of the deceased. The death is permanent. It is painful and involves many of the same emotions as divorce, but there are no hopes for anything in the present or future that involve interacting with the deceased. Divorce, on the other hand, is the death of a relationship, the death of shared dreams, the death of a family unit, the death of companionship, and so much more.

However, the person still lives and moves on to other people and other things and you are alive to witness it. The spouse is still around for conversations, disagreements, rejection, lingering hopes for reconciliation, and so much more, and these interactions and hopes can continue for a long time. When children are involved you are actually never able to completely remove this person from your life, especially if your ex is a good or at least decent parent who would attend major events in the child's life or special activities at the child's school. Even after the children are grown, there is the event of sending the children off to college—will both of you attend?

When a child gets married, generally both of you will attend the ceremony and one or both of you could bring a date. If grandchildren are born, perhaps both of you will be present at the hospital. Although the marriage has died and your relationship as a couple is over, if you have children you must at some point come in contact with your ex. If there were no children born into the marriage it can be easier to part ways and have no contact, but you will still grieve and eventually you'll move on emotionally.

People do grieve in different ways, but the underlying process is similar for most people. When you are going through a divorce, or have finalized a divorce, you have experienced the death of a relationship with someone who you love, or once loved, dearly. To say goodbye to all that you have shared is a huge event. Since this life-altering decision, has occurred, whether it was your choice or not, you will naturally grieve what will no longer be an intricate part of your daily routines.

Whether you wanted the divorce or not, grief will still be involved because everyone loses something in the divorce. Each person is losing something significant and both will experience a severing of two souls that were spiritually welded together in mutual consent. No one welcomes emotional pain, but when it is thrusted upon you or when a decision is made to end the marriage, you will experience some emotions. Often the marriage is ending while the couple is still together, so one or both is grieving the loss of the marriage before the divorce is finalized. Sadness, anger, denial, depression, and disbelief are all dealt with as you await the inevitable. You can know that the marriage is not going well and know that the marriage may not last, so your pain is being experienced while you are still together. Even though this is true, when you do finally divorce you will tend to still have some emotions to process once you begin to live in separate places.

Everyone may not experience all of the emotional phases of grief during a divorce, while others may experience all of them. The length of time each person grieves or stays in one of the emotional phases, or cycles in and out of the same emotional phase, is specific to each person. It has a lot to do with who left, if there was abuse in the relationship, how the relationship ended, and how each person relates to the other, which can sometimes be kind, indifferent, harsh, or even cruel. Many factors come into play when determining what feelings you will experience and how long you will go through the emotional rollercoaster of divorce. If you were the one who was left for another person, the rejection of being left for another person can be tremendous.

I can tell you that you will eventually feel better and the grueling pain that you feel initially will lessen as time goes by. Some people say that time heals all wounds, well if you do not work through the emotions associated with grief, you will not heal properly over time and will find yourself hurting longer, or you will experience the same types of emotional pain in new relationships. The manner in which you handle your grief during and after a divorce is truly important to you healing in a healthy manner and becoming emotionally whole.

Who wants to face emotional hurt or devastation? No one because it can be the most heart-wrenching pain and can often include an indescribable flood of emotions that can truly become overwhelming. Why is it necessary to face your feelings and allow yourself to experience them and not stuff them away and live life as if nothing has happened? Or why is it important not to move into a new relationship before you get over grieving the relationship you are in? It's important to process your feelings by acknowledging them and allowing yourself to express them. Working through each emotion you feel in a healthy way, as you experience them allows you to move through the grief process in a healthy manner. If you move into a new relationship while you are still hurting and have not resolved things from your marriage, you will be taking baggage into the new relationship and you might transfer how you are feeling about your ex to your new friend. The relationship could be a little rocky.

Both individuals will lose many things during a divorce. You will no longer share the same living quarters in most cases. I have known some couples who divorce, but due to economic challenges, they decide to stay in the home together but live separate lives. That, of course, presents another list of challenges as they attempt to coexist and see one another practically every day. But for the most part, when a couple breaks up, they lose companionship with each other. They may lose friends who they have shared because it may be too awkward for them or it may be too awkward for the friends. You may lose some family members of your ex whom you truly liked. You might lose economic support, and you will lose their presence in your life at social events. Perhaps you may lose your church family, as it may be too difficult to stay at the same church. There are so many losses when a couple splits, so it is natural to grieve what once was, even if you were miserable while you were together.

Emotional Phases During Divorce

What are the different emotions one might expect to encounter after a failed marriage? Common emotions include denial, anger, bargaining, depression, and acceptance. Not everyone will experience all five stages, and you may not go through them in this order. The emotions are generally looked at as phases of grief and they can happen in any order.

Shock and Denial

Denying that the marriage is over gives you time to gradually absorb the news and begin to process it. You might think, "he's just upset. This will be over tomorrow." This is a common defense mechanism and helps numb you to the intensity of the situation. This is your mind's way of protecting you from becoming emotionally overwhelmed.

If you were not expecting the divorce or did not want the divorce, you may find yourself in a daze wondering what is happening. You may feel numb and find yourself in a state of disbelief.

Anger

Anger is hiding many of the emotions and pain that you carry. You may be angry because you can't believe this has happened to you. You can't believe he would treat you this way. You may feel you hate him. You may feel that staying angry with your ex is a way to punish him. Prolonged anger can cause physical illness. You can let out all the pent-up anger that you shut off during the denial stage.

Depression

Then there is the depression and the tears and the lack of interest in the things you once enjoyed. Some days you may not want to get out of bed. You may lose your appetite. You just feel unhappy and don't know what to do about it. You could have problems concentrating or become irritable. These are some of the emotions that are experienced when a person is depressed.

Bargaining

No matter how much bargaining or negotiation you do with your spouse or in your mind, you won't be able to change what someone wants to do. He is who he is. During bargaining you are trying to convince the person why you should have stayed together, or what can be done to make things different. You may be trying to come up with some reasoning or rationale as to why he should ask if he could come back like maybe he'll miss the good meals you cooked for him or how well you managed the finances. Bargaining can keep you up at night running scenarios through your mind about how you could have done something better or how you can do things differently or thinking if his current lady friend was not throwing herself on him he would still love you.

If you are the leaver, the person who left the marriage, it is during this stage that you will either realize you've made the right decision or have made a mistake. If you left and felt it was a mistake, this is the stage where you will begin to pursue your husband. The important thing to learn during this stage is that you can't control the thoughts, desires, or actions of another person. The left-behind spouse—the one who didn't want a divorce—is likely to linger in this stage longer than the spouse who chose to divorce.

Acceptance or Integration

You've accepted that the life you shared—the marriage—is over. The obsessive thoughts have stopped, the need to heal your marriage is behind you, and you begin to feel as if you can have a fulfilling life. You open up to the idea of finding new interests. You no longer dwell on the past.

Guilt and shame can also be emotions you feel when going through a divorce. You can feel guilty if you believe you were the cause of the marriage failing. If you were involved in adultery or had an addiction and this resulted in the marriage ending you may feel guilty or shame because you feel you have let everyone down, the family or God. You can feel guilt and shame because you feel you have failed at being a good wife or parent and now your marriage has ended.

I went through a season of guilt and shame when my marriage ended. I felt I had let everyone down—my family, my church family, and God—and I was so ashamed because of all the lies that were being told about me, and they were lies. I felt I had let God down because I was unwilling or emotionally unable to change how I felt about things in the marriage. I started thinking maybe I should have just suffered through it, so for a while, I blamed myself and I was plagued by guilt.

My shame came from the church's view on divorce, especially of those in leadership positions. Everyone makes mistakes in a marriage because none of us are perfect. I owned my mistakes, gave them to God in prayer, and asked for forgiveness. I had to accept that I did not have to live my life in a manner that I believed was unhealthy for me. The truth is, if a marriage fails, both parties have a part in the failure, though one party will carry the majority of the responsibility for the marriage failing. Regardless of who carries the most responsibility you don't have to live in guilt.

How Should You Handle the Different Emotions?

Shock or Denial

If you find yourself in shock or disbelief, and things are not changing and your spouse is still moving forward with the divorce you must accept what is happening and what your spouse is telling you. Remember everyone has a free will and even if you fast and pray for your husband not to leave, he may still leave because God does not violate our will. At some point, if he leaves and is moving on you should accept his decision and work to move on yourself. If you refuse to accept what has happened, you cannot move forward.

Once you accept things are over, you may become sad, or even depressed, angry and then return to disbelief. You may fluctuate between disbelief and these other emotions for a while. People often describe their state of mind as confused and they have difficulty functioning normally. They forget things that are quite common activities that they have always performed. This is normal and will eventually change. Recognize that denial is common but eventually accepting what has happened or is happening is necessary for you to move on with your own life.

Depression

If you become too depressed and are unable to function or get out of bed, and this lasts for more than a week or two, you should seek professional help immediately. If you find yourself suicidal or homicidal, you should seek professional help immediately. These feelings are signs that something is going wrong and you need professional assistance to overcome these feelings. You can always call 911 or go to the nearest emergency room and tell them how you are feeling, and they will give you the adequate support that you need.

Take a few minutes to complete the Depression Checklist in the Appendix to do a self-assessment of how you are feeling on the depression scale. Professional therapists use this checklist to assess if a client may have some degree of depression. It can be a useful tool that you can refer to from time to time to evaluate your mood. It is a short checklist and should only take a few minutes to complete. There is a scale at the bottom of the form that shows you where you score on the depression scale. If your score is higher than eleven, please see a professional therapist, psychologist or psychiatrist to have an official medical evaluation. You may need additional professional support if you are feeling this way for more than a week.

There is a Difference Between Sadness and Depression

Everyone feels sad at some point, and people do cry when they are sad, or reflect on things that hurt them. Tears are good because they allow you to naturally release how you are feeling. They are a process that the body uses to cleanse itself of emotional stress, distress or hurt we are experiencing. So, do cry. Allow yourself to shed some tears and don't see it as a sign of weakness. Sometimes all you need is a good cry to get through the moment and you'll feel a load lifted. Your problems won't necessarily be solved, but you will have off-loaded some heavy internal weight that you have been carrying.

"I will not allow myself to cry over someone who has hurt me so deeply. She does not deserve my tears. I'll never waste my tears on such a horrible person." These are the words a client shared as we discussed his ex and how he felt so deceived. He felt as though this was a good thing. But if you don't express your sadness, emotions will build up inside of you and fester. Eventually these emotions will come out, and often in a manner that is not healthy for you or others.

Depression is something completely different. Depression involves a combination of feelings such as those listed on the checklist, feeling discouraged, lack of motivation, a loss of satisfaction or pleasure in life, loneliness, feeling tired, decrease or increase in appetite, loss of interest in sex, feeling suicidal, feeling like you would like to end your life, or having a plan to harm yourself. If at any time you are feeling suicidal or wanting to harm yourself in any way, please call 911 immediately or go to the nearest emergency room. They are trained to help you and can provide you assistance and support immediately.

Review the depression checklist from time to time when you are feeling down in the dumps for several days so you can gauge how you are feeling. Remember if your score is above eleven take action immediately. Get some professional help. A therapist or psychiatrist will know how to support you.

Anger

Dealing with anger is also a normal emotion. People get angry all the time. It's not being angry that is the problem, but it is how you handle the anger that may need to be evaluated. Yelling or screaming, calling your ex every derogatory name you can think of when you are alone, and letting off steam is perfectly fine. Judy said that she dealt with her anger by blaming her ex for everything that went wrong in her life. If she got a flat tire, it was his fault. If she was late for an event, she blamed her ex. If something did not work out as she anticipated, she would call him a name that felt good to her and blame him for what had occurred. This made her feel better and was a method she used to express her anger.

Journaling is often a good way to work through what you are feeling. You can write down how you are feeling, or what is going through your mind on any particular day to express yourself and relieve some of the tension or stress you are experiencing. Journaling allows you to see your problems in writing and can encourage you to find a solution. It allows you to process your thoughts and combat the circling thoughts going through your mind. Another good thing about journaling is you never have to worry about your journal judging you. You have the freedom of self-expression without inhibition. As you journal about your fears and hurts you are facing your emotions and this will help you become stronger. Repetition is good and builds emotional strength, so freely write about certain topics over and over again.

Talking with a good friend or relative who is a good listener and just venting about how you are feeling is also helpful. Talk about your anger or how sad you are or what you wish could or would happen. A good friend or relative will be able to listen and not judge you, but let you express yourself and respond in an understanding manner. Sometimes just having someone listen to you while you let off some team is therapeutic.

Try writing a letter to your ex and tell him exactly how you feel. Once you've written the letter, instead of mailing it, tear it up. This way you are releasing your feelings and not engaging your ex in an unhealthy manner. Even if you don't want to do it, do it anyway; self-expression is a vital part of your healing. Let's get all those unwanted feelings and unwanted thoughts out in the open. Maybe you want to call him names and say just how horrible he is or maybe you want to say how much you love and miss him and wish things could have been different. Whatever you are feeling and want to say write it in a letter to him and then tear it up.

Acceptance

Acceptance means you now realize that nothing can be done to fix the marriage. When you are in this final phase you will begin to view life differently. People set new goals and return to school, change careers, start a new business or relocate because their perspective on life is now different and their priorities in life have changed. Use this season in life to evaluate your opportunities, think about what you'd like to make happen for yourself. Dream big and then pursue your dreams. Many people indicate that after their divorce they tapped into talents and ambitions that were dormant for years. Some have said that their divorce was the best thing that could have happened to them.

If you did not want the divorce or did not see the divorce coming, your reaction to the loss will be significantly more intense and you will find yourself acting in ways you may have never imagined, or making promises to change or do things you normally would have never entertained. Why? Because the thought of losing the relationship can be so frightening. All types of thoughts and questions will run through your mind. What will I do? What will happen to me? How will I make it by myself? How will I survive without him?

You may have tried to get back with your ex because it is just so hard being without him. Not necessarily because you believed it was best for you, but because it is easier to be with someone familiar than it is to be alone and start over again. Lynette had been with her husband for about thirteen years.

He was irresponsible with money and had been unfaithful numerous times over the years. When he eventually left to be with someone else, as unhappy as she was, she begged him not to leave. She hated the way she was being treated, the disrespect she suffered, and the humiliation she had endured, as her friends knew of his escapades and disappearing acts. The pain from the loss of the relationship was difficult. She grieved the loss of the bad relationship because she did not want to be alone and was feeling the emotional severing of what was a part of her life for years.

With grief, you will experience numerous emotions that will come and go over a period of time. How long the internal aching or challenging emotions last is different for everyone, because all marriages are different. This can depend on many factors like, how long were you together, was the divorce unexpected, how committed were you to you husband, or is one of you in a new relationship do you have children together and how do you handle change? Some experts say you should give yourself at least two years while other studies say it takes about a year for every five to seven years of marriage to get over a divorce. So according to this study, if you were married for fifteen years, it will take about three years. Some people bounce back more quickly. There is no definite timeframe. The important thing to note here is that if you are willing to work through the difficult emotions in a healthy manner, you can heal and be healthy and feel good about your life. As you move on, you can be open to new love or, you can choose to be single, happy and satisfied with your choice in flying solo. You can control and you get to decide how you want to live life and what makes you happy.

Wherever you find yourself in the grieving process, be assured it will eventually end. Some people try to ignore the feelings and stuff them away as if they have not been fazed by the loss of the relationship. This is not healthy. A healthy way to grieve is to face your feelings, don't ignore them. Tell yourself this pain and all of the crazy emotions that you are feeling are only temporary, they will not last forever.

The different emotions associated with grieving the loss of a relationship can come and go at any time, sometimes when you least expect it. When going through my divorce, one day I was at home cleaning the restroom and listening to music. Then I looked in the mirror and just burst into tears. At first, I wasn't sure why I was crying, as I was happy to be out of the marriage. Yet I was crying, but what I came to know was though I had been unhappy in the marriage, I still missed the person I had been married to for eleven years. I missed the life we had together and some of the things we did together. I was grieving the loss of what we had and the dreams we shared. I was still hurting because it was over, and things would never be the same. I didn't see tears coming and I actually thought I was doing okay at the moment, but out of nowhere it hit me, some random memory crossed my mind and I was reminded that the life we had was over. The tears began streaming down my cheeks. It was actually over.

Many people believe that they will experience the different emotions in some type of linear pattern; one emotion after another and then it will be over. Sorry, but this is not true. We are not able to control what emotions we will feel first or last. Actually, the emotions are cyclical, and they are experienced in no particular order and can come and go many times during the grief process.

It is an awful feeling when you know your spouse or significant other has left you because he wants to be with someone else. Your self-esteem takes a big hit, your heart is broken, and the pain can be truly overwhelming. I was dating, I was truly in love with the guy I spoke of earlier and I thought I could change him. I had a young, naïve thought process that told me I was every woman and he would give up dating other women and commit to me, and he did for a long time. We were in love and had planned to spend the rest of our lives together. However, at some point he decided he wanted to see other women every now and then. How long this was going on, I'm not sure, but clearly it was in his nature to cheat and at some point, he decided he was moving on to be with someone else, because I was constantly in his face about it. I was crushed. Words cannot express the level of pain I experienced. I cried, walked around in a daze, and I felt absolutely horrible. The pain of a broken heart and the pain you experience when someone leaves you for someone else is excruciating, especially if you really liked or loved the person. There is nothing you can do to feel better or make it stop, you just feel awful for a long time until one day you realize "I feel better".

When I began working with Rene, she shared what took place in her marriage that lead to their divorce. Her husband of twenty-one years was having an affair with a neighborhood friend. She mentioned they talked initially, and she forgave him, and he agreed to end the affair. Then she found out he was still seeing his lady friend, and when she learned he had been in the relationship for over three years, she was devastated. She loved her husband and thought they were happy in the marriage. He begged her not to leave the marriage. They tried counseling several times, but she just could not get it out of her head. Nothing he said in counseling made a difference. She was angry and felt everyone who knew what had happened should be angry with her husband as well. She lost weight and was having panic attacks. If he left the house and was gone for a while, she would wonder if he was out seeing his lady friend. She lost all trust and respect for him.

She felt bad about herself because in her mind her husband had chosen another woman over her and was only pretending to be happy at home. Rene was the major breadwinner so she felt like a fool for giving him access to all her money for so many years. She mentioned that some days would be good and then without warning she would be so angry and start fighting and yelling and cussing. On other days she would just cry and feel sad. She wanted to keep their family together for their children, but she was not able to get over all the deception and betrayal that had taken place. After almost two years, Rene filed for divorce. She just did not see him the same and could not let go of the pain and humiliation she felt. There were too many lies, and too much hypocrisy. She said there was no way she could forgive him.

I worked with Rene for almost a year coaching her and helping her remain focused as she continued to grieve and rebuild her life. She wanted help getting past the failed marriage so she could move on with her life. She did the hard work and was willing to face how she was feeling and process those emotions. She eventually acknowledged some of the things she did wrong in the marriage and owned her part in things breaking down. She worked through feeling rejected and feeling unlovable and eventually realized and accepted that people cheat because they want to not because the spouse caused them to or because something was or was not done in the marriage.

If someone is treated badly or is emotionally or sexually neglected in the marriage, and chooses to have an affair because of this, they made that decision to have an affair not their spouse. A person has an affair because they found something they liked or desired from another person—period. Maybe they were or were not getting it from their spouse. It does not matter. No one is responsible for another person's behavior. We are all in control of our own actions, and if we do wrong we need to own it and not blame someone else for the wrong we chose to do. Neither should we blame ourselves for the wrong others do against us. Through time Rene accepted this truth and learned to love herself and even realized that the world is her oyster and in her words she is now living her best life, happy, single, dating, is open to love, and is advancing in her career in a different state.

Chapter 6

A TIME TO FORGIVE

"Then Peter came to Jesus and asked, 'Lord, how many times shall I forgive my brother or sister who sins against me? Up to seven times?' Jesus answered, 'I tell you, not seven times, but seventy-seven times.'"
– Matthew 18:21-22 (NIV)

I n the above quote from the New Testament of the Christian Bible, Jesus teaches his disciple Peter and others about the true nature of forgiving. The message we are intended to receive and understand from this passage is that everyone should have a heart to forgive. The focus is not on the seventy-seven times, for this is a parable, an analogy provided for how one should view forgiveness. The numbers merely signify that we should always forgive and that everyone at some point in their lives will commit an act against another person and will stand in need of forgiveness. No one is exempt. In the nature of building healthy communities and positive interactions among people, it is necessary for everyone to forgive because everyone offends and will find themselves in need of someone's forgiveness. To forgive is to release someone from a debt that was owed and the punishment they deserved—a pardon. Not because they deserved it, but because the forgiver was merciful.

Sometimes it can be difficult to forgive someone who has wronged you and other times it can be difficult for someone to forgive you for the wrong you have committed against them.

Why Is Forgiveness Important, and Is It Necessary?

In the context of divorce, forgiveness can be viewed in terms of how one spouse feels about the other. Is he worthy of being forgiven for what you believe was mistreatment, betrayal, or many other wrongs suffered during or after the marriage? First, let's look at what we mean when we say to someone "I forgive you" or "I'm sorry for what I did or said."

The Forgiver: To forgive means you are letting go of the hurt, anger, or disappointment that you have suffered from another person's actions.

The Repentant: If you tell someone that you are sorry for what you may have said or done, then you are asking them to accept your apology and not hold what you've done against you.

In both cases, there is an element of forgiveness. In one instance of forgiveness, if you say to someone, "I'm sorry for what happened," you are in essence asking them not to hold your wrongful acts toward them against you. You are hoping the damage incurred will be overlooked. When someone has treated you in a manner that has offended you, hurt you, or has caused some type of harm to you, you can decide whether or not you will hold them accountable for their actions.

Forgiving someone involves two or more parties. If you choose to forgive, then you are releasing the hurt, resentment, anger, and other ill feelings you have held within against someone. You are freeing yourself from internal agony, stress, ill will, and other types of negativity attached to the offense you suffered. So truly, when you choose to forgive someone, then you are allowing yourself to move forward and away from the hurt you suffered in the past. Releasing this pain is a freeing experience because you no longer have any negative energy bottled up within you because you have made a choice to let it go and move on.

If, on the other hand, you choose not to forgive, then you will hold onto that past event and you will carry it around with you. From time to time, you may feel the anger, resentment, sadness, or other emotions that have festered. The experiences will resurface, and the emotions will feel quite fresh because they have not been thoroughly worked through and you have not been able to heal from the experience.

My point is that forgiving your ex for any damage you have suffered will be for your healing and growth and not his. It is possible to hate and be angry with someone for years while they are moving on with their lives, maybe having a good time or even living their "best life" as the saying goes, while you are trapped by the horrible damage you have suffered.

Are They Being Punished?

Generally, when we have unforgiveness toward someone, we may believe we are punishing them, but are they suffering or being penalized by how you are feeling? Maybe, depending on if you have been withholding something they truly want but cannot have because you will not surrender it, as this is the punishment you have sentenced them with. Or maybe you will withhold the children from seeing their father because you are so angry about how he has treated you. Or you may speak ill of the father and tell the children about all the horrible things he has, done like not sending money and spending it on other women or gambling it away. Or you tell them that he is not sending the money because he does not love them and he is just punishing you and the children because he is evil and just an awful person. Or perhaps you tell them how horrible of a father he is, has been, or was while they were growing up. This could be your punishment for him. He will truly feel the wrath of your unforgiveness if these punishments are issued in response to the pain you suffered. So then, when it comes to the children and their father, if he has not physically or emotionally caused them harm how will the children benefit from hearing and believing these accusations against their father?

Their view of their father will be damaged, and their view of men can be framed in a way that they may not be able to have healthy relationships. If they are male children, what does that do for their self-esteem or self-image, if their view of their dad is negative, or if their feeling toward their father turned to dislike or even hatred? This will not be healthy for any child, and it would not be fair to them. A child deserves to have both parents in their life if it is possible, even if we disapprove of the decisions and choices their father is making or has made. Children are smart and they are able to form opinions of both parents by themselves. They should be given that opportunity and not have their view tainted because of the hurt you suffered in the marriage. It is not fair to them.

You also run the risk of the children resenting you for speaking negatively against their father, and you might cause a strain or a wedge in your relationship with the child or children. Unforgiveness can surely cause a lot of pain and a lot of damage if it is not dealt with and worked through in a safe and healthy manner.

For your well being and internal freedom, work through it and let go of the anger so that you can be free. To forgive someone does not mean you have to like them or be friends with them, it just means you are releasing all the bottled-up emotions you have stored up against the man who caused you harm.

Jennifer was married to a minister who was a chaplain in the military. She shared that she never knew she was capable of hate until her husband moved out, divorced her, moved in with another woman, took their children off the medical insurance and put the new woman's children on the insurance in their place. She could not believe he would deny his children the right to medical insurance. She was so angry. She felt hate in her heart for the first time because he was taking from their children health insurance that they needed. She did contact the military and worked through their system and was eventually able to get the children reinstated on the insurance and began receiving monetary compensation. She thought, "How could I ever forgive him?"

He was not worthy to be forgiven, and she did not want to forgive him. She held on to this resentment for years and every time she had to deal with him with regard to the children, the hatred welled up inside as if the incident had just happened. We discussed her feelings and she talked about being a Christian and understood that all Christians are to forgive a person who has wronged them because our heavenly father, for all the wrong things we have done in our lives, has forgiven us.

This unresolved offense was bothering her, and she wanted to know how to process the anger and be able to forgive. She confessed that she was so hurt by his actions that she did not know how to let it go. We worked through her anger in numerous meetings and discussed surrendering the pain and anger in prayer. This was not an easy task and surely would not be resolved with just one prayer. We discussed the art of meditating and being still before the lord as often as possible and letting go of all negative feelings and receiving his peace. While in prayer and meditation she would practice letting go of the anger and ill feelings. She would pray "Lord please take this hate from me as I do not know how to let it go" and she would visualize herself releasing it and giving it to God. She would also pray "Lord give me your peace, I receive your peace" and would visualize during prayer God giving her His peace.

Some other freeing exercises include writing letters to her ex that she would never mail, and journaling about how she felt. Eventually, she was able to release herself from the hate she'd been feeling and was able to consciously forgive him in her heart without ever having a conversation with him. Forgiving him was for her emotional healing. She was able to let it go and was no longer haunted by the past event that had lived inside, unsettled for years. She was free and was happy to let it go and not look at it the same again.

The father's actions to withhold medical insurance and financial support from the children were beyond selfish and irresponsible and showed a lack of concern for the well being of his children. Jennifer's feelings were understandable. I am thankful she was able to let it go and move on to better things. Forgiveness is a personal act, and each of us has to decide if we will forgive those who offend us. It is a personal decision and should be done in a way that is safe and healthy.

Sometimes it can be hard to forgive yourself if you know you did something wrong and caused harm or hurt to others. If you committed a violation in the marriage that caused your spouse to ask for a divorce that you did not want, you might feel guilt for the marriage ending. Maybe you had an affair, or you mismanaged the family finances and put the family in financial ruin, or disrespected your husband constantly until he could no longer live in those conditions, or perhaps it was something else. It can be a horrible feeling to walk around feeling guilty or responsible for the marriage failing. Some people are guilt-ridden and cannot overcome the burden they are carrying because it seems unforgivable.

Here is what Tammy told me when I began working with her. "I confessed to having an affair and he was so angry. I made no excuses for what I did because I knew it was wrong." She shared that she was hurting in the marriage and had endured a lot of verbal and physical abuse and wanted someone to care about her and how she was feeling. So in sharing with a friend, she became emotionally attached because she could talk about all the hurt she was feeling. She mentioned that it was not a sexual relationship, it was an intimate connection where someone listened and heard her and enjoyed her friendship without there being any sexual activity. However, they did eventually have intercourse, and she stated that sex was not the driving force of their friendship, but they did cross the line. It happened a few times, and she was guilt ridden. She could not live with the guilt so she told her husband to free herself of the anguish. He was angry and unable to forgive her, so he divorced her and she was not able to forgive herself.

Tammy felt a lot of guilt and shame and believed she did not deserve to be forgiven. She knew she had broken the marital covenant and hoped her husband would eventually forgive her, maybe seek counseling, but that was not the case. When I met her, she was guilt-ridden and needed help in working through what she felt was unforgivable. She took ownership of her actions against the marriage. I guided her in seeing how freely she was able to pardon others because she saw their humanity and understood people make mistakes. However, extending the same compassion to her was difficult. We worked through events in the marriage the good, the bad and the ugly, and we spent time reviewing how forgiving she had been towards her ex in the marriage.

We worked through her hurt and the loss of the marriage, and she eventually lightened up on herself admitting she was holding herself to a perfect standard that no one can attain. She revisits the many violations committed against her that she had forgiven. She accepted that she deserved to forgive herself just as much as she was willing to and did constantly forgive the ill treatment she received in the marriage. She apologized to her ex for the hurt she had caused him and eventually she let it go and forgave herself.

Some offenses are viewed differently than others depending on who is doing the evaluating and who is committing the offense. When we forgive ourselves, we accept the wrong that we have committed, the damage we have done, and the hurt we have caused, and we work hard to avoid making the same mistake in our current relationship and future relationships.

> "Forgiving does not erase the bitter past. A healed memory is not deleted. Instead, forgiving what we cannot forget creates a new way to remember."
>
> **– Lewis B. Smedes**

Chapter 7

BECOMING THE BEST ME

Building Self-Esteem and Self-Worth

It's now time to focus all your attention on you. In this chapter the focus is building you up and reinforcing a positive self-image. It takes a lot of hard work and commitment to work through grief. To combat all the exhausting emotional challenges and hard work you are doing to heal, it is important to balance your healing process by reinforcing and building your self-worth and self-esteem. It is important that you are able to feel good about yourself. If you are having trouble feeling good about yourself, there can be many reasons for this. It could be that you've always struggled with feeling confident or good about yourself, or maybe because of the failed marriage your self-worth has taken a plunge. Sometimes, after a failed marriage, you can become critical of yourself and blame yourself for the marriage not working. If your ex-husband left you for another woman, this might cause you to feel bad about yourself if you compare yourself to her.

Let's think about you, who you are, and who you will become. Thoughts can be powerful and life changing. Therefore, it is vitally important to control what you think about yourself and what you say about and to yourself. We will focus on the following action items that you will use to reconstitute and encourage yourself:

- Replace negative self-talk with positive thoughts
- Speak positive and self-soothing affirmations to and about yourself
- Create a vision board
- Get out and meet new people and do new things
- Create a "Count my Blessings" list
- Keep yourself healthy and take care of your body

It is easy to get in the habit of thinking negative thoughts or saying negative things about yourself and not even be aware that you are doing it. For instance, if you make a mistake or forget to do something or say something incorrectly, you might tell yourself, I'm so dumb. Or if you forget your work laptop at home and not realize it until you get to work you might tell yourself, I'm so stupid I can't remember anything. You might walk around thinking I'm always making mistakes. They are going to fire me. You may not realize how often you make these types of statements to yourself. But the more you speak negative things to yourself, the more ingrained they become. Too much negative self-talk can affect your mood.

Begin reprograming your thinking by replacing negative thoughts with a positive substitute as soon as you recognize yourself thinking the negative thought. You should practice talking back to these negative thoughts so that you can replace them with positive, rational thoughts. You must do this throughout the day, every day. If you tell yourself something long enough, you will start to believe it, and if you believe something, you will begin to act out what you believe to be true. You will need to track all the negative thoughts you have about yourself by writing them down. You can use a journal, notepad, or your computer to keep track of these. It is important that you stay consistent with this in order for it to be effective. Decide on a writing strategy that is easiest for you to maintain every day over the next several weeks or even months.

Make two columns and label them "Negative Thoughts" and "Positive Rational Response." By recording your automatic negative thoughts and replacing them with positive truthful thoughts, you are training yourself to think positive things about yourself. Repetition + consistency = permanency. Here is what it might look like. Example: I can't believe I forgot to pick up the milk from the store. I'm just worthless. I can't remember anything. This becomes Stop. I am valuable, and I remember lots of things. You can even list a couple of things you remember, like setting your alarm at night.

Self-soothing affirmations are good because these affirmations reinforce positive things you already believe about yourself. Work to reinforce positive beliefs that you already have about yourself. Things like, I am a good cook and people enjoy my food. I am a loving person and have some good, positive friends in my life.

In your journal you should be recording your grief work and your affirmations:

- Record how you are feeling each day as part of your grief work as discussed in chapter 5.
- Negative self-talk and the positive rational response you used to replace it.
- Daily self-soothing affirmations.

Meeting New People

Begin thinking about getting out and meeting new people and making new friends. You can join a new group or club; take a yoga or zumba class or take a continuing education course. You can meet new people in these types of settings. Broadening your social circle and Interacting with new people allows you to discover new things and move out of your comfort zone to explore new things with new people.

Treat Yourself

Treat or pamper yourself by doing nice things for you. Think about what feels like pampering and then plan some pampering time at least once a month. If you have time add in a few more in the month. You might consider going to a spa and getting a massage and enjoying the hot tub and sauna. At home you could take a nice bubble bath with a few candles around and the lights dimed. Have some of your favorite music playing and your favorite beverage and relax and enjoy the moment. Treat yourself to a movie or a delicious meal at a nice restaurant or do both. Go to a concert or to see a play or to an opera. Treating yourself is about doing things you like. I've given you a few ideas but you can use my list and add some of your own ideas to it. Remember it should be a treat; something you don't do regularly. Make it special and select something that will make you feel good. It's all about you!

Count Your Blessings One by One

Make a list of all the things you are thankful for, no matter how small. Sometimes when you begin to reflect on what is going well in your life, you can drown out the loud, negative thoughts that want to tell you how nothing is going well for us. Things like, I am thankful for a roof over my head because some people are sleeping under a viaduct fighting off rodents.

Or I am thankful that I am able to think sound thoughts and dress myself each day. These are blessings we often take for granted, but our lives would be extremely different if we did not have them. Choose something small or something big it doesn't matter just make sure you choose something. Create a list and when you are feeling kind of down, think about all the things that are going well. Add to this list weekly and read it

Make a Vision Board

Make new goals and start thinking about how you want your future life to look. Write down some short and long-term goals. How would you like things to look in your life in the next three, five, or ten years? Let's start planning. Use the following information as a guide to create a vision board.

1. Perceive your intentions.
   - What do you want?
   - What do you need?
   - What do you value?
   - How do you want to feel when those things are your reality?
   - (When thinking of the feelings, choose words like free, open, joy, etc.)
2. Gather your supplies. Here are some ideas for the type of supplies to gather:

- blank art book with mixed media paper
- poster board
- a large sheet of paper
- a cork board
- index cards etc.
- get some glue, clips or pins to adhere your images
- markers, pens, pencils, paint, crayons
- paper, white or different colors
- magazines and books that you can cut or tear up
- scissors

3. Find a Special Place.

    You should dedicate space where you are comfortable and able to spread out your supplies. Use the floor or a table as your workspace. Next set up the area in a way that creates a sense of comfort and relaxation so you can tap into your inner desires. You might like some music playing, or candles, or something else to support you getting into a relaxed mood.

4. Get Images and Words.

    Gather some pictures, words, images that resonate with your intentions or goals. Check online, look in books or magazines or create your own on. Gather a lot and then we will narrow them down to a smaller selection.

5. Select your favorite items from all that you have gathered and attach them to your board.

Choose what truly resonates with you, images that produce the feelings associated with your intentions and invoke positivity and good vibes. If looking at an image makes you feel like I'll never have that or I'll never get there then don't choose that image. You want to select the items that give you a sense of happiness and security. When you look at your board you should feel as you described under your intentions.

6. Place your vision board in a location that is visible.

You can use your vision board as a visual reminder of how you want to feel, your personal core values and your intentions. Look at it often. You can look at it daily or once a week. If you'd rather pull it out when you view it then place it somewhere out of sight and retrieve it when you are ready to view it. Remember to look at your vision board often.

7. Make a right now list.

Write a list of things you can begin doing right away that is in sync with your intentions.

You want to begin living in alignment with your values and intentions. I call this living on purpose when you let your core values guide you. Make a list that involves doing things that involve you taking action and things you can control and not things you'd like others to change or do because the only person you can truly control is you. Your list should include things that involve: your thoughts, feelings, emotions, choices and actions. What things can you begin today?

8. Observe—Heal & Move Forward

This is where you put theory into practice. As you are begin bringing your vision into reality, you will encounter some road blocks that manifest in the form of stories, beliefs you have that limit you, unhealed emotional wounds, habits, or unconscious patterns. This is to be expected as personal transformation is always met with obstacles and challenges. As you begin to live on purpose you will work through the resistance and change your limiting beliefs into obtainable realities. Working through these challenges contributes to you fulfilling your dreams and creating a fulfilling life.

9. Continue to move forward.

Evaluate your progress periodically and make adjustments, as you are moving forward. Stay on course, don't relent and you will reap the benefits of your consistency and intentional actions. The vision board is your visual reminder of things you desire and how you want your new life to look.

Reinforce Your Affirmations

Another thing to do is to speak your affirmation to yourself when you're driving in your car or doing housework, while taking a relaxing bath, and as you are falling to sleep at night.

Keep Yourself Healthy

Staying healthy is very important and you may tend to ignore your physical health if you are not thinking clearly. The stress associated with divorce can manifest surprising ways. Pay close attention to what your body is telling you. Some of the stress symptoms are headaches, stomach problems, rashes, muscle aches, grinding teeth that can lead to dental cavities, tweaked muscles, and heart palpitations. Watch out for these symptoms and take some time to address them. If they persist, make an appointment to see a medical provider.

Some people loose their appetites when under a lot of stress and others eat for comfort. So pay attention to when you have last eaten a health meal and be sure not to spend the entire day without any food. If you find yourself eating for comfort, purchase some healthy snacks and avoid bringing too many unhealthy foods home, you can't eat what you don't have. Focus on nutrition and if necessary force yourself to eat something healthy every day.

Working through difficult emotions can cause you to pick up destructive habits so be cautious and pay attention to any new habits that may being trying to form like excess drinking or too much sleeping or not sleeping much at all. Monitor your daily habits to observe any big changes that may be forming. If you notice a change, talk to your doctor to see what you can to improve these unhealthy patterns. Remember to take your medication if you have any medical concerns, eat healthy meals, and make and keep your well-woman checkups.

Journaling

Continue to record what you are thinking and how you are feeling each day so that you have a way to evaluate and reflect on what areas in your life are still unresolved. Including the positive rational responses to your critical self-talk, allows you to maintain a balance as you heal and move on with your life.

Chapter 8

WHAT'S BEST FOR
THE CHILDREN?

"It is easier to build strong children than to repair broken men."
– Fredrick Douglas

"We worry about what a child will become tomorrow, yet we forget that he is someone today."
– Stacia Tauscher

"Mess with my children and I will fight you like a thug in the streets."
– Freda Wilson

Your children are the innocents during your divorce process, and they should be protected at all costs. They are incapable of processing what is seen and heard from the most important people in their lives. Children will often feel that they are the reason for their parents separating and divorcing, so it becomes vitally important that we talk with them based on their ages. It can be difficult working with your children if you are in the middle of an emotional breakdown and you are unable to care for yourself when devastated by a divorce.

This is the time to call on all of your immediate support figures, family members, and friends. Perhaps your mom, dad, sister, or a friend can come to stay with you for a while to support you with the children. If no one is available, hiring someone temporarily is another good option. Perhaps there is a good neighbor who can assist you for a few hours a day. Be willing to do what you must to ensure that your children are not suffering and experiencing any emotional or physical harm as you and their father are figuring out how to restructure your new lives apart. What's vitally important is that you take care of yourself and make sure you are well, mentally and emotionally. If you are not taking care of yourself, you will not be able to give your children all the good nurturing, love, and support that they need as their nuclear family unravels.

Depending on the age of the child, they will not be aware of anything that is going on, but small children do need love and nurturing while you work through the difficulties of divorce. Infants and toddlers may not know exactly what is happening, but they can understand security, consistency, love, and nurturing. It is important to reassure our young ones by hugging them often and speaking with them in calm tones and maintaining a consistent routine so that their sense of security is not disturbed.

Preschoolers and young school-age children may understand the word "divorce," but they are more interested in some of their primary needs and have questions like:

Where will I stay?

Am I going to be left alone?

Where will my stuff be?

When will I see Mom?

When will I see Dad?

Do you still love me?

They are more interested in knowing why you are getting a divorce, and over time the questions may become more challenging. Do your best to be honest and share information in a way that is appropriate based on the child's age. How to answer questions about what to tell their friends will require some assistance from you so that they are able to respond in a manner that is helpful for them with their peers.

For school-age children, it is good to explain what is happening in a manner that they can understand. Let them know that Daddy and Mommy are going to be living in separate houses. Reassure them of how much both of you love them. Answer any questions that they may have that may come up in the coming days or weeks. Be sure not to speak ill of the other parent and continue to reassure them of how much they are loved.

Teenagers will generally want the most information and an honest answer should be given but with limited detail. It would be inappropriate to give children the details of what has taken place between you and your husband during the marriage. Always remember that they are your children and not adults and not your friends.

One of the challenges mothers will face is inconsistency with child support. I highly recommend working with the court systems to receive any financial support you should receive from your ex during and after the divorce. Going through the courts is not an attack against anyone; it is a security system you can put in place to ensure you receive financial support for your children. Your children deserve to have the lifestyle they've known maintained as much as possible. If your spouse was the major wage earner and the children will live with you the majority of the time, the financial support or medical insurance should be determined immediately or as soon as possible. If you were the major wage earner and financial support is to be given to your ex for the children, do what is right for the children, even if everything within you does not want to give any money to him. Remind yourself that this is for the children, so that they can be cared for as well as possible when they are away from you.

If you have to give spousal support to your ex, based on the financial calculations that are determined under the law, try to remain reasonable and work within the guidelines of the law and provide the amount that you are legally required to pay. I know this may be difficult for many women, but these are the laws that have been put in place to protect and do what is fair for all. The majority of the time, men are responsible for the child and spousal support during separation and divorce, and we expect them to step up and do what they should. On many occasions they hate that they have to give what has an amount that has been determined by law, so it becomes a huge battle in court to get what the spouse and children are entitled to receive. Some women walk away and just give up. Be strong and do what is best for you and your children.

I worked with a mother once who was the major wage earner and the husband was on full disability, receiving assistance from the government and prior employers. When looking at him, he did not appear to be disabled. He worked with the children as they trained in their sports, washed the clothing, and kept the house clean. He was a stay-at-home dad. This was the arrangement they established for their family, and they were okay with it. It worked for them.

When the wife found out that her husband had been involved in an affair with a family friend for years, she nearly lost her mind. All attempts to work through the pain of the infidelity and the issues he complained of that led to him going outside of the family failed. She could not overcome the depths of deceit and hurt. They tried counseling several times and they all failed. She was unable to get over the betrayal and the idea that he chose another woman over her. She was having panic attacks, was full of anger, and became violent with him. Other times she would just cry and ask why and how could he have done this to their beautiful family? No answer he gave was good enough. The children witnessed many of her verbal and physical assaults against him, and this went on a little over a year before they separated and decided to file for divorce.

They both got lawyers, as they could not agree on the division of assets and the retirement. She did not want him to have half of everything. She felt that it was his fault that their family was destroyed, and he should not want her money as he had disability income that she would never be entitled to because that is the way the law is established. Eventually, she had to concede because she had no legal grounds to withhold what the law states a stay-at-home spouse is entitled to, regardless of the sexual affair.

So much money could have been saved if, after being advised, she would have just agreed and let the fight go. Thousands of dollars paid to lawyers when, in the end, he got half of everything. Now some women do believe that a man should not take money from women; they live by the traditions within which they were raised. No one is above the law and we must do what is required whether we agree with it or not.

I have also witnessed numerous occasions where the father does not want to give the mother what she is entitled to under the law. I've known men to hide money in accounts under a friend or relative's name and hide property that they have purchased or owned in other states. One woman said she never knew how much her husband made. He paid the mortgage and she paid the utilities. He never kept his financial information in the home, so she had no idea what he did with his money. She was employed and worked outside the home, but she was also responsible for taking care of the home and the children.

Her husband would disappear for days or weeks and come home with no explanation. She threatened to divorce him many times, and each time he convinced her that he would change, so she stayed because she loved him and wanted her family. But once he convinced her not to leave, it was not long before he was up to his old habits of not coming home some evenings and living as he chose. When she finally had enough, she got a lawyer and began divorce paperwork. She looked throughout the entire house trying to find any financial records, check stubs, or bank statements, but found nothing.

Then one day she thought about where would he might keep this information, and she decided to look in the trunk of his car. In it, there was a box of financial records, check stubs, bank statements, and information on property that he had purchased. She secretly took photos of everything and shared this information with the lawyer. Once the records had been legally researched and verified, additional searches were made by her attorney to ascertain if there were other assets that had not been uncovered.

They made their financial requests, based on what they were aware of, and the husband was livid, thoroughly angry that she was aware of his financial secrets and was adamant that she would not receive a penny. After his threats and outbursts, which he soon figured out, were having no results, he decided to ask for reconciliation. She refused, as she knew from previous attempts at making things better that he would not change. He was now only concerned with losing his things. Through lengthy court proceedings, she eventually received half of all the marital assets and financial compensation for herself and the children, based on the laws of the state where they resided.

Of course, the children were not spared from the challenges the parents faced during the rocky periods of their marriage, and so they have emotional scars that will manifest in their lives because they were not spared the ugly fights their parents engaged in while living together and going through the divorce. In the earlier family mentioned, the children told their parents they needed to just divorce if they were going to continue to live together in such an unhealthy manner. On multiple occasions, the son would get in between them to stop his mother from hitting his father and would say, "Why don't you hit me? Why do you keep trying to fight him?"

Once he could not take it and he picked her up and slammed her into the folding closet doors and they fell off the hinges.

Do what is best for the children. Don't expose your children to such harmful, unhealthy patterns of living. Remove yourself from any violent environment and seek help if you are being physically assaulted. And do what is legally necessary to remove the children from any environment that is unhealthy. They are not able to protect themselves from their parents' actions. It is up to the parents to make decisions to protect the children, despite the pain, fear, or other emotions you may be experiencing. They depend on you to do what is best for them.

Mark and Shelia were separated, and every other weekend Mark would pick up the children to stay with him for the weekend. When they were back home with Sheila, they would casually talk about things they did while with their dad, and on one occasion it was mentioned that one of the men from the church had spent the night over at their dad's with a few friends. What the kids did not know, but the mother did, was that the man had been previously accused of molesting his children and had spent some time in jail as he was charged and found guilty. He had always insisted that he was innocent, and the accusations were untrue, stating the children were lying because they did not want him chastising them, so they told their mother he was abusing them, and she believed them. I don't know if the charges were true or not, but he was convicted and did go to jail. Therefore, the mother was rightfully angry that the father would allow someone with this history to sleep in the same home with her children.

The father did not understand and believed the man was innocent, so he felt there was no harm done. The mother felt it did not matter whether it was believed or not, she did not know the details, so her only concern was to protect her children from any potential harm. She let the father know that if it ever happened again, she would report him to the authorities and take him to court for child endangerment. She insisted that the children were not to be around this individual and under no circumstances should he be allowed to sleep in the home when the children were there. Doing ministry and helping restore others from past tragedies is good work for adults, but there must be a line drawn when it comes to children and it is best to err on the side of caution than to potentially put the children in harm's way.

Mediators

To save a lot of finances and drawn-out legal proceedings, it is often a good idea to work with a professional mediator who charges a lot less than what can be spent going to court with lawyers. Judges are not mediators. An agreed-upon mediator can help in recommending what is fair, based on the information that is provided by each party. Oftentimes, the mediator can work with each parent in a separate room and work through the negotiations without either of you having to experience difficult behavior or intimidation that may come from one of the spouses. If you are able to work together with a mediator, you can save yourselves a lot of time and finances that can be put to better use. To find a mediator in your city, search for Divorce Mediation and the name of your city using Google. For example, "Divorce Mediation Chicago." You can also visit one of these sites:

https://www.equitablemediation.com/blog/how-to-find-a-good-mediator
https://www.adr.org/
https://www.mediate.com/mediator/
https://apfmnet.org/

When it comes to visitations and the children having to go over to their father's house, try to keep yourself out of the details while you are still healing. You may experience different emotions, like maybe fear that they'll love their dad more than you. Perhaps they will have more fun with their dad, since you are having to do all the structured tasks like keeping up the daily routines such as homework, getting them to school, preparing meals, and keeping up the laundry and the home all alone, and if you work, you may have little energy to do many fun things. It will be important to create fun times and happy memories with your children, even if that means some of the daily maintenance in the home has to be put off for another time.

Allow your children to see you laugh and being light-hearted with them. Do fun things like playing games, going to see a movie, or spending time in the park. Make space for them amidst all the responsibilities you have to juggle. It will increase the bond between you, and it will create good memories for them as they grow and mature. Always remember that more is always caught than is taught, so be mindful and intentional about what is done with them and around them.

When it comes to dating, your ex-spouse may bring a lot of different women around the children and this can be a difficult challenge for you and them. What they are learning and being exposed to when they are not with you is important. While we cannot control what the other parent does and how he lives his life, we can insist on healthy activity and behavior. You can always consult an attorney to determine what parameters can be put in place when it involves who can care for the children when they are with their father and what activities can and cannot be prevented. The attorney will be able to advise you on what can be done legally to keep the children from learning too much too soon, and to protect them from being left with too many different individuals whom you may or may not know.

Generally speaking, we cannot control whom our exes choose to date and when they are introduced to the children. Sometimes the children may hurt when they see one of their parents with someone of the opposite sex in a romantic way, but this is sometimes inevitable and should be handled by you in as mature of a manner as possible. One woman said she was so angry to see her ex parading around with one of her previous babysitters, as if everything was peachy keen. She was so angry, but there was nothing she could do about it. He chose to date the babysitter, and though she hated it, it was still important to communicate with her children about these types of activities in a manner that was best for them. Each situation is different and thus will have to be handled based on what you are presented within your situation. Lots of prayer and consulting with wise friends or a professional will help you in dealing with these types of situations in a way that is best for you and the children.

I always recommend that you not bring a lot of different dates or interested parties that you are getting to know around your children. It's best to keep your dating life and activities to yourself until you are seriously considering making a significant move into a relationship. This way you don't have to get the children involved in any emotional ups and downs. We will discuss more on dating in Chapter 9.

Chapter 9

BUILDING RELATIONSHIPS

If you think you are emotionally ready to start dating, then give it a try. Dating can stir up some emotions, so be sure that you have done the hard work of putting the past behind you. You don't want your unfinished business to spill out into the new friendship because something was said that reminded you of your ex and you didn't respond in the best manner. If you find yourself constantly speaking about your ex, this is probably an indication that you may still be holding on to the past and need a little more time to work through some things to fully leave the past behind. Take a break, continue with your journaling and writing down how you feel, saying your affirmations, and treating yourself well. You'll get there, and you'll know when the time is right.

I've had many people say to me after a difficult divorce that they do not want to get married again. It's too much work. But after some time has passed, and they have worked through the difficult period of emotional ups and downs, most have said, "Okay, maybe if I find the right person." In most cases, finding the right person does take time, though some have had the fortunate opportunity of meeting their new love soon after the emotional roller coaster ended. This is generally not the norm, of course. If you are considering a serious relationship again, you can prepare yourself by putting a few things in place before you start.

First, think about the type of person you desire to spend time with. Since you are not emotionally entangled with anyone, your mind and emotions are free to consider what works best for you and the type of person you are most compatible with. If you make a list after you are involved with someone, the list can get skewed because you may make concessions for the person you are seeing because you want it to work. With the freedom to be selective, ask yourself what your top three "must haves" are in a companion. These top three are traits that you cannot live without. If they are missing, it is a deal-breaker. I would caution you against having a list of superficial things, such as "must drive a sports car" or "must have green eyes." These items would be nice if this is what you like, but they have nothing to do with the character or values of the person or how you would interact or what they could add to the relationship. There is a difference between needs and wants. For this list exercise, the first set of items would be your "needs" list. If you don't have your needs met, you will not be satisfied or fulfilled in the relationship and it is more than likely that it will not work. Here are a few of my top "needs" when I started dating again:

1. He must love God; not just go to church, but also have an active relationship with him and desire to live a life that is dedicated to him. He doesn't have to be a scholar, but must have a genuine love for and relationship with our creator. Clearly if I'm in ministry to teach people about God and life with him, my significant other must have a similar value to be compatible with me.

2. He must love children because I have children, so anyone that does not love children will absolutely not work.

3. He must be educated—this item is more important to me than he must have a lot of money. I'm attracted to people who are intelligent and not arrogant and who value education.

These were the top items and if they were missing, I did not even consider the person as an option. See what I mean?

Keep in mind, you can have more, perhaps five, depending on what your needs are.

Next, you should make a list of things you would like to have but are not deal-breakers. Now you can get into other items that are not necessarily deal breakers, but they would surely be nice to have. Make a list of about five things that would be nice assets for your companion. When you are getting to know new people, you can easily get the answers to your questions in general conversations. You don't want to conduct an interview. This will be a turn off for a lot of people. I had one lady tell me that a few of her dates felt like they were being grilled or interviewed because she was asking so many questions about them. Take it easy, and in general conversations you will be able to ascertain the things you are looking for.

If after getting to know someone, you know they are not a fit, be sure to put the brakes on when it comes to other outings. No need to waste your time or theirs if he's not what you are looking for. There's always a polite way to get out of spending time with someone. Now, if you are not looking for a long-term relationship and you are just wanting friends to do things with and nothing serious, you don't have to be as strict with your needs and wants because you are not looking for any type of commitment.

Everyone has values and they are important standards to keep, so when dating or getting to know people, don't allow yourself to go against your value system. A value is a strong belief that you have regarding what is acceptable or important. Some examples would include things like honesty, diversity, faith, loyalty, and generosity. If you share the same or similar values with someone, that is a good indication of compatibility as you value some of the same things. Knowing your core values will help keep you grounded and true to whom you are, and the things that are important to you. It's important when dating to not be influenced to go against your belief system or the things you value in life. Once you begin doing things that are against your values, you begin to lose who you are and what's important to you.

Boundaries are another important factor when interacting in a relationship. Boundaries are good because they establish rules or guidelines in the relationship and allow you to be comfortable and capable of saying yes or no to requests, or not allowing others to violate things that are off-limits. It is your prerogative to have limits and personal space. Establishing boundaries can be uncomfortable, especially when someone is trying to convince you to change your mind about something.

Here's an example of how you will establish a boundary. Let's say you know you have a deadline to meet at work and must spend the next two evenings working on it to complete it on time, but your guy calls and says, "Hey, I'm going to bring the kids over. Will you watch them for me? I have a couple of things I need to take care of."

You adore the children, but you know they require a lot of hands-on attention that will distract you from completing your deadline. In order to accomplish your goal for work, you would respond, "No, I'm not able to do it tonight. I have some deadlines I'm working on, and it can't be late."

Perhaps he persists and asks again, "Come on, this is important to me. I need you to come through."

You would repeat yourself and just say, "I can't."

More detail is not necessary because you don't want to get caught up in a lot of back and forth. If he asks a third time, "Please, I'm going to be disappointed if you let me down. I need this."

You would respond, "No, I can't. Actually, I need to go now; I have some things to finish up. Talk with you soon." And say goodbye. You remain polite, but firm on your decision. Eventually, it will be understood that your no means no.

I had a young lady share with me that her husband put so many demands on her. If he was in school, then she was in school, meaning she was required to help him with his papers or assignments even if she had other things planned. What she had planned was not important to him because his school was first since he was doing it for the family. It did not matter if this demand came at the last minute, she was expected to change her schedule and help him. If she said she had other plans, he would get angry and begin to tell her why she was wrong and being selfish.

She soon realized that she had not established any boundaries with him, so whenever he had a crisis or emergency, she was expected to change and make adjustments or undergo some lengthy verbal assaults about how she was letting him down. Since he did not understand boundaries, he thought his request or demands were just normal expectations. There is nothing wrong with helping your significant other with schoolwork, surely that happens with couples. Papers are edited, assistance is provided with equations and such. The difference is that the requests are not demands, and if there are other pressing things, it is okay if the spouse is not able to assist at that moment.

I like how my girlfriend would tell her son, your lack of planning does not become my emergencies. Boundaries are healthy, and they build a sense of mutual respect in the relationship. When setting boundaries, you have to be willing to let someone be angry when you are setting limits that are new. Be careful when setting boundaries and make sure you don't become too inflexible. Having balance is always a good standard to keep. For example, say you wanted to stay home and just relax for the evening. Perhaps you had a long day at work. Your significant other calls and he mentions he was thinking about seeing a particular movie and needed to get out of the house because he had a bad day at work. He wants to clear his head by enjoying a good movie and would like it if you could join him. You have a couple of ways you could respond. If you are tired, you could say, "No, I'm just too exhausted." Or if you hear in his voice that he is down and could use some cheering up, or just some time with you at a movie to help ease the pressure, you could say yes. Both answers are okay. One just listens more in a concerned manner, and if it were possible and not causing any harm for you, perhaps flexibility would help someone you care about. See the difference?

Euphoria in a dating relationship makes everything seem like heaven. It happens often for some people. Boy meets girl and things are going well, they have a lot in common and they enjoy each other's company. Talking on the phone is so exhilarating and soothing, so they might tell themselves this is the one, though they've only known each other for about three weeks.

I know a guy who has this reaction often after meeting someone new. He'll call and say, "I've met someone, and she is everything I need," and he'll describe their interactions and how things have been simply bliss since they first met. Then, about a couple of months later, he says that it didn't work out, but the week before he thought he was in love. What happened? Eventually, the newness of the relationship wears off, and people begin to see each other in less hyped interactions. Some different aspects of their personalities are discovered. Habits and idiosyncrasies are noticed and perhaps some disagreements are encountered. Eventually, one of them decides that it's not working for them, or they're looking for something a little bit different and so the whirlwind romance ends. What happened to the guy I knew? He was moving too fast. He got so caught up in his emotions and his desire to have a long-term relationship that he did not take the time to get to know the person before he put his heart out. He moved much too fast because he was anxious to be with someone.

Generally, when you initially meet someone they are on their best behavior and putting their best foot forward. I heard one comedian say you are meeting their representative. They say what they think you want to hear, and they do what they think you like because they are trying to make a good impression. It takes time to let all the facades fall off before you see some of their other characteristics, like how they handle conflict, or how they are when they are with family and friends. Letting the newness and euphoria wear off before you invest your whole heart is wise. There is a great proverb that says, "Guard your heart with due diligence because out of it flows the issues of life." In other words, be careful when choosing who you will give your heart to because as you know, when that heart gets broken, it can feel like the life is being sucked out of you. Proceed cautiously.

Another thing women tend to find themselves doing is assuming the relationship is more than what it is. If the person is treating a lady nicely, calling frequently, and you are spending a lot of time together, of let's say five months, do not assume that you are his "only" lady friend if these words have not come out of his mouth. If you want to know if you are exclusive at some point, be sure to have that conversation so that you know where you stand.

I recall an incident where a friend of mine, Earl, a nice guy, was a bachelor and he was looking for the "one" as he would say. And he indicated he would know when the right person had come into his life and made him want to settle down. He dated plenty of women with no strings attached, and everyone knew the nature of the friendship. Generally, they did not last long or did not spend a lot of time together on a regular basis, maybe once a month or so.

Eventually he met a young lady that he liked, and they had been seeing one another for several months. He mentioned that she might be "the one." I asked if they were exclusive and he said no. I asked if she knew that they weren't exclusive, and his response was, "I have never told her that I was not seeing other people, so she should not make that assumption." Based on previous conversations he and I had about their relationship, I told him, "She is probably thinking she is your only lady friend, so if she finds out she is not, she will not be happy."

Sure enough, the time came when she was visiting him that she noticed items in his home that indicated he was seeing someone else and she was upset. They argued and he made his little speech, that he never told her that they were exclusive so why would she assume that. Her response was, "I am not that type of person," and she took her things and left upset. He had to decide if he wanted to give up being single and free to live as he wanted, or if he wanted to settle down. He did have strong feelings for her and they were very compatible. Eventually, they did discuss things, and he made the transition from being fancy free and they became an exclusive couple.

You get the point I am making. Don't assume the relationship is more than it is. Perhaps you don't want to be tied down, so be clear about the type of friendship you have when you are spending significant time with someone. If you are getting to know people with the intentions of having an exclusive relationship that will move into marriage, have that conversation to see if he has the same goals. Some people don't want to get married. They just want casual relationships where they treat each other nicely and with respect, but they are free to make independent decisions and go out with other people at will.

One young lady met a guy who she enjoyed spending time with, but he was not looking for marriage and she was. He wanted to remain single with no commitments. Since she was newly back into the dating scene, a year and a half after she and her husband broke up, she was okay with that because she wanted the freedom to meet other people and just enjoy being flattered and treated like a lady. He had a little more baggage in his life than she would have liked for a long-term relationship, but she did enjoy the time they spent together. They talked often, and spent a lot of time together, but they were both clear that they were free to date other people, and they remained respectful and considerate with one another. The key here is to be clear about what you want and don't want. Don't make assumptions about the commitment level, have a conversation, and make sure everyone is on the same page. If you want more out of the relationship than he does, decide if you should move on or still see him from time to time. If your feelings are hurting because he does not want the level of commitment you want, you should think hard about moving on so that you can prevent yourself from feeling bad or getting hurt. Don't limit yourself. Take your time and get to know people.

When is a good time to start having sex? This can be a tricky question and it has a lot to do with your values and what you are looking for with this person. If you are truly looking to find someone to grow with in a long-term relationship, I would suggest holding off on sexual intercourse because your judgment can get skewed. You can get so emotionally tied up into the physical aspects of the relationship that you are not able to check out the person for who he is. Sometimes when you become physically intimate, you tend to think you have more in the relationship than is there, so I say proceed cautiously and exercise wisdom. If you are a Christian and endeavor to live according to the teaching of the bible, then of course the teachings are that you should abstain from having sexual intercourse outside of marriage. Use good judgment and always practice safe sex.

I always recommend getting to know people before you move into a committed relationship. Give yourself an opportunity to see and do different things. You've spent a lot of time in a marriage and healing from that breakup, so take your time before you jump in with both feet. Don't be anxious, there are plenty of fish in the sea. If you have children, it would be wise not to introduce the children to everyone you date. Some people may only be around for a short while, so no reason to bring the young people into the picture. You want to make sure he is someone worthy of meeting your little darlings. I dated my current husband for almost a year before he ever met my children. We talked about our kids and shared photos, but I wanted to see if he was going to be around for the long term. It turns out he was a keeper, and my children truly love and respect my husband, and he loves and respects them as well. Of course, nothing is guaranteed, and sometimes things don't work out, but at least you'll have a plan for how you want things to unfold as the relationship progresses.

Chapter 10

REDEFINING YOUR LIFE

God is a God of love. He is good and his mercies endure forever (Psalms 100:5). Our creator is not like humans. He is not fickle-minded and neither does he throw us away. He loves everyone, but of course not everyone loves him. I'd like to suggest that this might be because they do not know him or understand him; therefore they cannot love someone they do not know.

Divorce is not the unforgivable sin. God does hate divorce (Malachi 2:16). His desire is that two people joined in marriage would commit to one another and live their lives together in mutual love and respect and in reverence to God.

However, people have always strayed away from God's best. Jesus teaches in Matthew that marriage was intended to be a lifelong commitment, but due to the rebellious actions of many against the fidelity of marriage, allowances were made for people to get divorced. This however was not part of God's original plan (Matthew 19: 3-6,8).

When a Christian chooses to divorce, a decision is being made to act against what God desires. She may suffer some of the natural consequences associated with her actions, and these will be different for each person because all circumstances are different. Speak to God about your decision to leave the marriage and ask for his forgiveness. If you confess your sins, he is faithful and just to forgive you of your sins and cleanse you of all unrighteousness (1 John 1:9). If your husband divorced you when you did not want the divorce, then he is responsible for his actions, not you. If the marital covenant was broken, the offended is not required to stay in the marriage. They are free to leave, though not required, and move on with their life and are acting in accordance with biblical teachings.

If you were married to a pastor, or church leader and were hurt deeply by things that occurred in the marriage, I can imagine your wounds may be deep and you may have many questions. If your trust has been damaged and your beliefs are now in question, spiritual healing is necessary for you to recover in a healthy manner. I've known several women who were married to pastors and the pastor decided he no longer wanted the marriage because the wife was no longer desirable to him. Many have had affairs and sometimes these affairs are no secrets to other leaders or members of the church. It can be hard to recover spiritually when your "pastor" who is also your husband is guilty of numerous violations against you. Particularly if you really believed in him and thought he was not capable of some of the things you experienced.

Now to be fair, I've also known pastors' wives to have affairs, perhaps for different reasons, but still a violation against the marital covenant. What do you do with your hurt and how do you overcome the disappointment and betrayal? Is it possible to have the same pure trusting feelings you once knew? What are the wounded to do and what is God saying about all these things?

For the wounded, you must know that all men and women are human and are tempted with the same types of sin, and leaders in the church are not exempt. They too have to fight against fleshly temptations that will steer them away from what God desires. Leaders are held to a higher standard (James 1:3) because they have accepted a call to live above reproach and be an example for the people they lead. They are to lead by example and will be accountable to God for their actions (Hebrews 13:17; 1 Timothy3: 1-4).

To heal from hurt received from your ex who was or is a leader in the church, here is something to always remember as you heal and move forward with God. *Always remember that God is the only one who deserves your complete trust. Never put any leader on a pedestal and view them as incapable of doing things that are clearly in violation of scripture. Leaders are respected for their teachings and their labor of love among us, but we are not gods.*

To all followers of Christ, here are some practical steps you can take to heal from the pain of divorce: Allow yourself to heal by removing yourself from any church that is unhealthy and hindering your spiritual growth. If your church is healthy and a good place for you to be natured and healed, consider limiting your level of involvement and too many obligations so that your focus can be on healing, hearing the word and growing. If you are without a church home, find one immediately. Find a place of worship where the teaching is good and the environment feels emotionally safe and helpful. You may have to visit several churches before you find the church that seems right for you, but don't grow weary, continue to look. You will find a place. Ask God to lead you. Everyone should take notes and plan to review what you have heard in the coming days. Don't be in a hurry to get involved, take your time to hear the teachings, absorb them, and listen to what God will say to you. He will provide guidance through the preaching and teaching of the Holy Scriptures. At least once a week, preferably more often, carve out personal time to meditate on the teachings you are receiving and to pray and connect with God in solitude, perhaps in a room with soft Christian music playing and away from all distractions. In a posture that is comfortable for you, pray and share all your hurts and pain and ask God all your questions. Ask him to heal you and to take away the pain and renew and strengthen your relationship with him. Remain there for a while in silence and continue to clear your mind if you become distracted by unrelated thoughts. Listen for what God may whisper in your spirit. Anything you believe God is speaking to you will always line up with the teachings of scripture. If you are unsure, your pastor or leaders in you church should be able to help you discern what you are sensing.

Be open to forgive to free yourself from the burden of carrying around bottled up emotions. See the chapter on forgiveness. Share your feelings with other faithful Christians who are mature in the faith and are able to support you through the healing process. Remember, God loves you and he wants what is best for you. He'll never give up on you. Lean on him as you heal, and he will strengthen you and enable you to move forward in renewed confidence.

Chapter 11

WHEN THE HEALING GETS TOUGH

Healing properly takes time, discipline, and determination. Imagine you broke your arm in several places, so you go to the hospital to get it repaired and instructions on what to do for the pain and to have a fully functioning arm once it heals. In order for this to happen, they have to break your arm again because it has started healing on its own, but improperly. If they do nothing, your arm will mend in a deformed manner, the bones will not be properly aligned. You agree to allow them to break and reset the broken bones so that it can heal properly and be fully functioning once it has completely healed. After the bones have been broken and realigned, you experience a lot of pain, and a cast is placed on your arm to keep it stabilized for several weeks to ensure proper healing.

If the cast is removed prematurely, you run the risk of the bones moving and becoming misaligned and causing it to look abnormal, compromising full mobility of the arm. You agree to the process and keep the cast on, and you keep your arm in a sling throughout the day to ensure proper healing. To function through the pain while the arm is healing, you are given instructions to take pain medication several times a day and instructed to restrict your activities until the cast is removed. After a few months of complying with the doctor's orders, the cast is removed and your arm looks a little thin, but you are able to move it and the pain has subsided.

Just as the physical body has to be nursed and assisted to heal when bones are broken, your eternal body, your soul—mind and emotions—has to be nurtured and assisted when you have been wounded or broken emotionally from a failed marriage. You must be guided through the healing process to ensure that you heal properly and are nurtured. Prescribed exercises and instructions are your medication that will help you heal properly. When you are feeling the pain from the wounds and the flood of different emotions associated with your grief, you may become overwhelmed. The assistance I've provided in the chapters of my book will help you stay on track and continue to heal in a healthy manner. Not working through your emotions properly can delay your healing and cause you to stuff the emotions inside to avoid them. Avoiding the pain and not processing the varying emotions can lead to bitterness, resentment, anger, and depression and can adversely impact your ability to build healthy relationships in the future, as well as impact your ability to return to complete healthy functioning and interaction with others. You may start lashing out at the children or having anger outbursts with the people close to you. If you become depressed and are unable to pull out of it, your daily activities and routines can be adversely impacted.

To stay on track with your journey to wholeness, here are a few things to look for, identify, and push through so that you can stay on course and continue the work necessary for healthy healing.

Obstacles

You may want to resist reaching out and asking for the help recommended in Chapter 3: *Getting the Help I Need*. Avoid ignoring the recommendation to have a few people or family members you can call upon to talk with and assist you with caring for you and with the children, if applicable. This support in your life is a vital part of your healing. You must be able to share how you are feeling. You will need someone to be real and transparent with, so that you don't keep the emotions and pain bottled up inside. You don't want the pressure to get so high that you explode in ways that could be harmful and inappropriate.

Remember, a support group for individuals working through divorce or a professional therapist are also options if you don't have friends or family you can call upon who can identify with what you are going through or be the nurturing support you need.

When you are feeling different emotions, you may be tempted to try to avoid them by ignoring what you feel. If you keep them locked inside, you can't process them and if you don't work through them you won't heal properly. Resist the urge to not do the work, push your way through the different emotions. It may be painful and exhausting, but it will be so worth the work in the end. Remember to do the journaling as you face your pain and differing emotions. Describe what you are feeling, try to identify why you feel a certain way and write it down. If you have a solution for something you've been dealing with write it down. Write, write, and write, whatever the thoughts or feelings, just write. When you are at a settling point, write how you want to feel, some positive emotion that you want like joy, serenity, or love. Then, write down some positive affirmations as we discussed in Chapter 4: *Becoming the Best Me*.

Forgiving someone is a difficult challenge. It can be even more challenging if you believe the person does not deserve your forgiveness. And forgiving yourself can be difficult. Think about the heavy load of ill feelings inside—anger, bitterness, hate, and resentment—these emotions you are carrying around with you every day, they are you hurting you.

The tendency to ignore this portion (forgiving) of the healing can be tempting because you may feel they or you don't deserve to be forgiven. Ask yourself why, and let's add these feelings to the journal. If you are feeling stuck here, consider reaching out for some spiritual support or a professional therapist. Remember, forgiveness does not mean you have to be friends with someone. You don't ever have to see or speak with the person again. Restoring interaction is not the point and neither is it the goal. Freedom from your past is the focus. The act of forgiving is a personal choice, and you have to first want to forgive to move forward. When dealing with abuse, you should reach out for professional support so that you can move cautiously through this. See Chapter 3: *Getting the Help I Need* to revisit the different types of professional support.

Don't skip Chapter 6: *Becoming the Best Me*. This chapter is extremely vital in building yourself up so that you are feeling great and able to thrive. You may get tired of the routine and not want to do this every day, but the repetition is what makes this work. Avoid the temptation to excuse yourself from the exercises in the chapters, they're important to building up your self-image and confidence.

Our children are our most valuable treasures. Don't slip up and bring them into all the drama. Even if you are feeling lonely, avoid leaning on your children and venting to them about your ex and all the hurt you are feeling. The temptation may be strong to vent about all the bad things their dad has done or how he is hurting you or neglecting them. Don't do it. Don't paint a negative picture of their dad to them. Let them form their own opinions. You want them to be protected as much as possible from all the ugliness that can come with a divorce, and you want to give them a fair chance at believing in marriage when they're older and considering having a family.

Being too close to someone too soon can be a stumbling block to your healing. Move cautiously when thinking about dating and revisit the teaching in Chapter 8: *Building Healthy Relationships* for some handy tips when you're ready to date. Getting involved too soon can pause your healing because you may want a mate to avoid grieving you ex, and you may end up in a rebound and wake up one day and say, "I don't like him." It's common for people to run to a new relationship to make themselves feel better. Be strong. Move slowly.

You may think carving out personal space to replenish yourself spiritually is not necessary. Even if you are not a Christian, taking time to de-stress and relax in solitude can be replenishing and is healthy emotionally and physically. With so much activity in our busy lives, you may find it hard to get away from the noise and focus on your spiritual growth and well being. Spending time in prayer and reflecting on biblical teaching will strengthen you. Avoid the temptation to put nourishing your soul and spirit on the back burner. Make it a priority. It is so worth it.

When you are always helping others, it is easy to avoid doing what is good for you. Don't ignore yourself. Put you first. You deserve to feel good about yourself and to feel happy. Take the time necessary to do what is best for you. Don't let anything hold you back, girl. As my daughter would say, "Chop, chop, get to it."

Chapter 12

I'M MOVING ON

I worked with Candace about six months ago and she is happy and enjoying her new life. She was able to do the healing work and reestablish herself as a thriving single female. Meet Candace. Candace, a practicing attorney divorced her husband after eight years of marriage. They had been having problems for several years. Her husband required a lot of personal attention and would complain about her not being a supportive spouse if she did not abandon everything she had planned and help him with whatever his needs were at the moment. They would have this problem when he would tell her at the last minute he needed assistance. If she told him she had to finish up a few things before she could proof a paper, or assist him with some other schoolwork he would fuss and complain for days telling her how he needed to be her priority because he was doing things to improve the family. Whatever she was working on was not important if he had a need that he wanted addressed.

Since her husband was from an abusive family where mental illness was present in his primary parent, functioning in chaotic situations was his sense of normal. If there was nothing going wrong and things were peaceful, he would start an argument or bring up something or say something that would cause them to have long drawn out discussions that would last for hours. He blamed her for all the problems they were having and complained how she was doing nothing in the marriage. He indicated the only thing she had done positive in the marriage was get up and going to work every day.

I asked Candace what positive things she believed she brought to the marriage and she mentioned the following: I helped him complete two college degrees. I proofed his papers, I helped write many of his papers, I helped him with numerous math problems, I read and interpreted legal documents during his law suit, I took care of his mother who was ill and visited her when he did not, I cooked his meals, washed his clothes and kept the house clean and that intimate stuff you know—smooch smooch.

Her husband had been under a lot of pressure at work and eventually was asked not to return because he was unable to get along with upper management. This caused more stress on the marriage and from what I could ascertain from Connie he may have been suffering with depression.

The marriage continued to deteriorate as he began spending time away from home and building a friendship with a female that Candace felt was inappropriate. When he decided he would stay out all night and not come home for several days, Candace decided the only way they would have a chance at the marriage working was to receive counseling. So she told him he could not come home until he agreed to marriage counseling. He refused to get help for their marriage stating he needed to focus on himself and he did not have time to work on the marriage. They never went to counseling. He never apologized for staying away for several days, and he never came home.

Candace did not know where her husband was living. He refused to tell her. Through a little detective work, she discovered he had moved in with the female she had been complaining about. Candace was really hurt because she did not want a divorce but what could she do as he was not willing to work on the marriage. This went on for several months with him calling mostly when he needed something but not to work on the marriage.

I began working with Candace while they were separated as she was hurting and was not sure what to do. She worked through my 8-step method for "Healing The Wounds of Divorce". As we worked together she eventually realized he was never going to work on the marriage and had no intentions of returning home.

She grieved for several months, almost a year but she continued to do the grief work to process her emotions. She was sad, sometimes angry, sometimes in disbelief and even did a lot of mental bargaining. She worked through her grief with a lot of journaling, as she loved to write and it help when she was feeling sad or really angry.

She had a girlfriend and a few family members both males and females that she would talk to often when she needed to make sense of things and when she just needed to talk about all the craziness that had been going on in their marriage. She found herself repeating the same things over and over again when she would talk with her family members. This was helpful because she was processing and healing.

She eventually forgave her husband and hoped he would get some personal counseling to work through his own personal issues. She really did love him, but she was not willing to accept the disrespect, and cheating. Enough was enough she said.

The affirmations and positive self-talk were very instrumental in helping Candice not feel down about herself when she thought about her husband living with another woman. She focused heavily on this method, as she needed it to remind herself of all her positive traits, and to balance the grief work she was doing. She did a lot of praying and bible reading and attended church often. She also joined a gym and began working out to relieve stress and to interact with other people.

Eventually a little over a year, Candace was ready to accept that her marriage was over and she had no desire for reconciliation. She concluded the marriage was not healthy for her and she moved on emotionally. She could actually think and talk about the marriage without having painful feelings. She filed for divorce about two years after their separation, after she had finished grieving and was sure she was no longer emotionally connected to their relationship. The divorce went smoothly and she was open to dating.

Candace decided to date casually for a while and not get too serious. She just wanted to have fun and have the attention of the opposite sex. When she met someone new, she would find out right away what they were looking for in a female companion to see if it aligned with what she wanted. She was keeping her options open but was content living single and enjoying herself. She was healthy and enjoying her life again.

Candace is a great example of what doing the grief work and other methods in the program consistency can accomplish. If you stay the course and take your time you will heal and feel good about yourself and your future. Be sure not to rush into a fully committed relationship without fully evaluating what you want and who the person is. It could take months to really know someone's true character. If you notice deal breaking characteristics, conflicting values or behavior you do not like don't ignore those signs. Don't waste your time just move on. Something better is waiting for you.

Healing our wounds after our marriages have ended is a challenging process and it takes time and patience. While in process, you may often feel as though things are not getting better and that you are just stuck in a state of no return to a sense of normalcy that is familiar. The truth is, this phase of your life will end. How it ends will depend on you. Dealing with the pain and flood of emotions, being lonely, feeling like you are going to lose your mind, the crying spells, the anger, the unending repetitive thoughts, can truly be overwhelming, but remember, these emotional challenges mean you are grieving and if you are doing the work you are also healing. Your body, soul, and spirit are working through the grief. You have suffered the death of a relationship with the person you pledged your life to, and now your dreams with this person have ended. As you go through the chapters you with learn methods to aid you in healing in a healthy manner as you move on with your life.

Remember how vital it is to reach out for help and allow others to support you through the grieving process of your broken marriage or relationship. Having the right support structures in place is truly essential for your journey to emotional well being. Choose the support systems that work best for you. Everyone is different, and you know what system of support you will receive the most strength from, so take your time to think about your options and then make some choices. Don't grieve alone. Allow others to hold your hand and be there for you. You deserve the support; so don't deprive yourself of this help no matter how awkward it may feel for you. Do it for yourself, you are so worth it.

Working through all the crazy emotions and knowing what to do and how to work through them is a huge portion of your healthy healing. It is hard work, but work that you should not avoid. Avoidance pauses the healing and can cause you to become bitter, mistreat those you love, or harm yourself.

You don't want to move on and into new relationships with a lot of unfinished business. The divorce rate for second marriages is higher than the divorce rate of a first marriage. If people don't allow themselves to work through their emotions and leave the ill feelings in the past, they will bring all the old baggage into a new relationship. Do the work, learn how to heal and be healthy, and you will move on to better things.

Forgiving someone or even forgiving yourself can be difficult, so I provided you with some practical ways of getting over the anger and letting go of the negative emotions that want to stay bottled up within you. You have learned how to work through and free yourself from the internal negativity couched in unforgiveness, so that you can free yourself from all the entanglements of your ex and past marriage. Forgiving allows you to say, "I won't be held back from moving on with my life." Understanding what it means to forgive can empower you to release all the negativity bottled up inside and knowing that forgiving does not mean you have to be in communication with some, if you decide not to, can be quite liberating.

After all the hard work of facing your emotions, building and replenishing your self-image and self-esteem balances this work. Your affirmations, positive self-talk, self-soothing and vision board are good image and life building techniques that are important to you believing in yourself, dreaming big and hoping for great things in the future. This is so important! If you feel good about yourself and what you are doing and where you are headed you will attract positive things. Building confidence and feeling good about you is a recipe for success.

The strength you use in protecting your children will be rewarding as you watch your children grow and mature because you have made the best decisions for them during a difficult time in their lives. They will be glad you did and will have a better chance of building healthy relationships in the coming years.

Putting new intimate romantic relationships on hold while you heal is healthy and wise. As you implement the strategies laid out for you, you'll be familiar with the type of mate you want, and you will know what the deal-breakers are when you meet someone new. Learning to set boundaries in a relationship, knowing what your "must haves" are in a mate, and not ignoring your personal values will aid you in choosing the right person to date and with whom to consider building a long term relationship.

Taking the time to focus on your spiritual growth can be so refreshing, replenishing, and life giving. Invest the time to allow yourself grow mentally, emotionally, and spiritually, the result can be thoroughly rewarding.

I recommend that you read this book a few times and reference it often focusing on the areas that address the needs you should tend to right now. Balance is essential. Healing and dealing with your hurt while you are actively building yourself up is a rhythm that moves you forward in inner healing and new life building. Take your time and work through the strategies I've outlined for you.

Working through grief is hard work but don't give up, keep pressing forward. Remember to honor your personal values and beliefs and remain true to who you are. If you decide to remain single, or if you choose to date or if you choose to pursue a new relationship don't compromise who you are. Continue the course you've started and you will receive all the benefits that come with living wisely.

"Healing the Wounds Of Divorce" 8 step program is offered online and in person.

CONTACT INFORMATION

Phone: 619-761-2228

Freda@helpenterprise.com

https://helpenterprise.com/healing-the-wounds-of-divorce-8-step-program/

Appendix

DEPRESSION CHECKLIST

THE BURNS DEPRESSION CHECKLIST*

Place a check (√) in the box to the right of each category to indicate how much this type of feeling has bothered you in the past several days.

	0 Not at All	1 Somewhat	2 Moderately	3 A Lot
1. **Sadness:** Do you feel sad or down in the dumps?				
2. **Discouragement:** Does the future look hopeless?				
3. **Low self-esteem:** Do you feel worthless?				
4. **Inferiority:** Do you feel inadequate or inferior to others?				
5. **Guilt:** Do you get self-critical and blame yourself?				
6. **Indecisiveness:** Is it hard to make decisions?				
7. **Irritability:** Do you frequently feel angry or resentful?				
8. **Loss of interest in life:** Have you lost interest in your career, hobbies, family or friends?				
9. **Loss of motivation:** Do you have to push yourself hard to do things?				
10. **Poor self-image:** Do you feel old or unattractive?				
11. **Appetite changes:** Have you lost your appetite? Do you overeat or binge compulsively?				
12. **Sleep changes:** Is it hard to get a good night's sleep? Are you excessively tired and sleeping too much?				
13. **Loss of sex drive:** Have you lost your interest in sex?				
14. **Concerns about health:** Do you worry excessively about your health?				
15. **Suicidal impulses:** Do you have thoughts that life is not worth living or think you'd be better off dead?				
Total score on items 1-15→				

THE BURNS ANXIETY INVENTORY*

Place a check (√) in the box to the right of each category to indicate how much this type of feeling has bothered you in the past several days.

Category I: Anxious Feelings	0 Not at All	1 Somewhat	2 Moderately	3 A Lot
1. Anxiety, nervousness, worry or fear				
2. Feeling that things around you are strange or unreal				
3. Feeling detached from all or part of your body				
4. Sudden unexpected panic spells				
5. Apprehension or a sense of impending doom				
6. Feeling tense, stressed, "uptight" or on edge				
Category II: Anxious Thoughts	0 Not at All	1 Somewhat	2 Moderately	3 A Lot
7. Difficulty concentrating				
8. Racing thoughts				
9. Frightening fantasies or daydreams				
10. Feeling that you're on the verge of losing control				
11. Fears of cracking up or going crazy				
12. Fears of fainting or passing out				
13. Fears of physical illnesses or heart attacks or dying				
14. Concerns about looking foolish or inadequate				
15. Fears of being alone, isolated or abandoned				
16. Fears of criticism or disapproval				
17. Fears that something terrible is about to happen				

*Copyright © 1984 by David D. Burns, M.D., from *Ten Days to Self-Esteem*, copyright © 1993.

THE BURNS ANXIETY INVENTORY* (continued)

Category III: Physical Symptoms	0 Not at All	1 Somewhat	2 Moderately	3 A Lot
18. Skipping, racing or pounding of the heart (palpitations)				
19. Pain, pressure or tightness in the chest				
20. Tingling or numbness in the toes or fingers				
21. Butterflies or discomfort in the stomach				
22. Constipation or diarrhea				
23. Restlessness or jumpiness				
24. Tight, tense muscles				
25. Sweating not brought on by heat				
26. A lump in the throat				
27. Trembling or shaking				
28. Rubbery or "jelly" legs				
29. Feeling dizzy, lightheaded or off balance				
30. Choking or smothering sensations or difficulty breathing				
31. Headaches or pains in the neck or back				
32. Hot flashes or cold chills				
33. Feeling tired, weak or easily exhausted				
Total Score on items 1-33→				

RELATIONSHIP SATISFACTION SCALE*

Place a check (√) in the box to the right of each category that best describes the amount of satisfaction you feel in your closest relationship.

	0 Very Dissatisfied	1 Moderately Dissatisfied	2 Slightly Dissatisfied	3 Neutral	4 Slightly Satisfied	5 Moderately Satisfied	6 Very Satisfied
1.Communication and openness							
2. Resolving conflicts and arguments							
3. Degree of affection and caring							
4. Intimacy and closeness							
5. Satisfaction with your role in the relationship							
6. Satisfaction with the other person's role							
7. Overall satisfaction with your relationship							
Total score on items 1-7→							

Note: Although this test assesses your marriage or most intimate relationship, you can also use it to evaluate your relationship with a friend, family member or colleague. If you do not have any intimate relationships at this time, you can simply think of people in general when you take the test.

Use your score as a guide to indicate if support should be received in improving intimate relationships.

A score of 0–10 = Extremely Dissatisfied

A score of 11–20 = Very Dissatisfied

A score of 21–25 = Moderately Dissatisfied

ACKNOWLEDGMENTS

While writing this book, two of my immediate family members are suffering life-threatening heart conditions and my husband, is experiencing spinal and hip complications. This has been an enormous weight on my heart, as I love each of them dearly. My Auntie Mother and husband are doing well and continue to improve. Unfortunately, my eldest sister Leslie whom I was extremely close with died suddenly, a few months ago, 2 months after a major surgery. Everyone including surgeons and other docs thought she was out of the woods and recovering well. My family and I were devasted and continue in our season of mourning.

I must thank my amazing husband Dr. Raphael J. Wilson for encouraging me to persevere in writing forward and always encouraging me in all I set my mind to do. Thanks for being my biggest cheerleader. I am so thankful for the love we share and the life we have built together. You are always my calm and my rock when the storms of life come. I love you dearly my love with all my heart! You are irreplaceable!

Dr. Angela E. Lauria, thank you for your vision for the Author's Incubator. It is because of your vision and wisdom that I was able to write this book. You provided the framework and guidance that I needed to get this book out of me and penned on paper. I am forever thankful.

To my editor Cory Hott you are an amazing person and a jewel of an editor. Thank you for your labor of love in overseeing the editing process for my book. You have been a huge encouragement to me during this entire process. I am so glad I was able to work with you. Thanks for all your editorial support, keen insight, and ongoing support in bringing this book to life. You are truly appreciated.

Thank you to David Hancock and the Morgan James Publishing team for helping me bring this book to print.

To my sister Leslie, thank you for always being there for me and in my corner during all my life adventures. Thanks for helping me brainstorm on a book title and thanks for helping me with some of the last-minute editing. Thanks sis!

To my sister Bridgette, thank you for all the emotional support you have provided. You had all the correct words I needed to hear at just the right time.

To my niece Tamara, thank you for helping me brainstorm on book titles and for the lengthy dialogues we shared while I was writing. Thanks for all your help with editing some of the chapters late at night and thanks for all the positive encouragement you gave me. I am so blessed and happy to always have your support. Love you girl!

To my darling children Dana II (Monet), John, and Angel, you are God's precious gifts to me. Thank you for loving me. Thank you for working through the challenges divorce brings on young children. You three are troupers and I am so proud of each of you. You have blossomed into remarkable adults. You are mama's best blessings. Hugs and kisses my loves.

To my nephew-son George (Miriam) and my niece-daughter Veronica (Juan), thank you for your love and for believing in me enough to receive my input in your lives especially on matters that mean a lot to you. Thanks for the last-minute proofreading Roni. I love you two dearly and the babies to the moon and back and then some.

To God be the glory! Most of all I thank God for providing and sustaining and taking care of me throughout all of my life. I'm so grateful! Thank you Lord, for guiding me as I wrote this book. I hope and pray that many lives are touched and healed. Without you lord nothing is possible! With all my love!!!

THANK YOU!

I appreciate each and every one of you who opened this book and committed to reading it from the introduction to the conclusion. You rock.

As a thank you, I've created a free mini-training that will provide more encouragement and support. Sign up at https://helpenterprise.com/healing-the-wounds-of-divorce-by-freda-wilson.

ABOUT THE AUTHOR

Freda Wilson is a native of Chicago, Illinois, and resides in San Diego, California, with her husband, Dr. Raphael J. Wilson, MD. She is founder and CEO of HELP Enterprise Inc., a social outreach organization that provides ministry and services for holistic success. She received her undergraduate education at Lincoln University and her bachelor of science degree in computer information systems from DeVry. She has two graduate degrees in ministry, a master of biblical studies and church administration from Logos Graduate School and a master of arts in applied ministry with an emphasis in global and contextual studies and community ministry leadership from Bethel Theological Seminary. She also has a certification in premarital and marriage counseling from Bethel Theological Seminary.

As a survivor of Chicago's inner city, the divorce of her parents, and other adversities, Freda has a profound sensitivity to the hurts and struggles of all people. She is an ordained minister and has over twenty years of experience working with individuals and couples.

Freda came to embrace the word of God, accepted Christ as her Lord and Savior, and was baptized in the Baptist Church. She embraced her call to ministry at the age of twenty-five and was licensed and ordained as a minister to spread the truth of God's word. She has served the Body of Christ in various manners, including co-founding and pastoring a rapidly growing community-based church. Further, she developed, implemented, and conducted a weekly radio and television bible teaching broadcast.

CPSIA information can be obtained
at www.ICGtesting.com
Printed in the USA
JSHW021820260121
11240JS00003B/73